THE
UNICORN
IN THE
SANCTUARY

THE
UNICORN
IN THE
SANCTUARY

THE IMPACT OF
THE NEW AGE MOVEMENT
ON THE CATHOLIC CHURCH

By
Randy England

TAN BOOKS AND PUBLISHERS, INC.
Rockford, Illinois 61105

TAN BOOKS AND PUBLISHERS, INC.
P.O. Box 424
Rockford, Illinois 61105

1991

TO MY WIFE

THE UNICORN

One of the most common symbols that New
Agers use as an identifying device is the unicorn.
The unicorn is a symbol of New Age transformation:
a symbol of destruction and renewal. This
mythical animal has often been associated
in literature with both Christ (wrongly)
and with Lucifer. It is not the cute
and gentle creature popularly
portrayed...but a symbol
of tearing and trampling,
of breaking and crushing.

Table of Contents

THE
UNICORN
IN THE
SANCTUARY

Foreword

When C. S. Lewis wrote of the distasteful task of writing his popular book *The Screwtape Letters,* he described the job of getting inside the devil's head as "all dust, grit, thirst, and itch. It almost smothered me before I was done." Any survey of the New Age Movement is likewise "dust, grit, thirst, and itch," but with a difference: the corruption is masked by a welcoming veneer. The material is at once revolting and enticing, blasphemous and seductive.

To live is to know sorrow. Intolerable poverty and starvation, cruelty, murder and war are widespread now, as always. This sick world screams for an answer, a leader, a solution to its predicament. "For we know that every creature groaneth and travaileth in pain, even until now." (*Rom.* 8:22). The New Age Movement promises hope for peace. Hope for a better life. It appeals to man's sensuality, for in the New Age Movement there is no sin as we know it—and more important, no guilt. Finally, and even more energizing than appeals to sensuality, the New Age Movement entices the proud with promises of power and of godhood.

The New Age Movement holds out all these things, but at a price, a price that Our Lord warns us is no bargain: "For what doth it profit a man, if he gain the whole world, and suffer loss of his own soul? Or what exchange shall a man give for his soul?" (*Matt.* 16:26).

As recently as 1980, few had even heard of the New Age Movement. Now nearly everyone has. Related movements or labels are: Human Potential Movement, Modernism, New Thought, Globalism, and the Aquarian Conspiracy. Parts of it include Mind Control classes, the Holistic Health Movement, Transcendental Meditation, Humanistic Psychology, Positive Confession, Feminist Spirituality, Positive Mental Attitude, the New Physics, and numerous political organizations, as well as various esoteric, environmental and animal rights movements.

I had heard of many of these before, but in 1983 I first learned from a radio program how they were tied together into a single whole. Author Constance Cumbey, who has since produced two books on the New Age Movement, was speaking about her research on the Movement. The story was, to me, incredible, but at the same time seemed to fit the facts. Soon after, I found the book *Peace, Prosperity and the Coming Holocaust* by cult expert Dave Hunt and read it through the same night. In finishing, I was both electrified and skeptical. It was all too big, too encompassing and too unbelievable, so I resolved to be vigilant as to its influence— but to avoid the awkwardness of sharing with anyone else that which I had barely begun to believe myself. My resolve lasted not twenty-four hours.

The next evening, I sat down to dinner with a friend and soon found myself regurgitating all that I had read. I told him about how occult teachings had been incorporated into the fabric of our institutions; into politics, into the churches, into business and sports. I told him about courses that teach people how to control their minds so as to control every aspect of their lives; how these teachings were strikingly similar to Nazism; how they are anti-Semitic, anti-God and anti-Christian. I told him how most of the writings of the Movement had been produced through automatic writing by which spirits allegedly speak through the authors. I even explained that many New Agers actually had spirit guides with whom they had frequent contact while in altered states of consciousness and that these "guides" ruled their lives.

My friend became quieter as I talked on for at least an hour. Finally becoming convinced that he thought me mad, I stopped and waited for some response. He had asked no questions and now looked at me grimly.

He said, "You haven't told me anything I don't already know." I restrained my surprise as I waited for him to go on.

"Last week," he began, "my mother filed for divorce from my father. She belongs to a group connected with our church. Each person in the group has two spirit guides which come to them while they meditate. The guides supposedly give you advice and help you with problems. One of my mother's guides is Jesus. Her guides had been wanting her to get my father involved with the group but he is not interested, so they ordered Mom to leave him. That's how I know about the New Age Movement."

From that point on, I began to research the Movement and quickly found that many individuals in my own church had deep involvement, both in the present and in the past. In showing the avenues that the Movement has paved into the Church, I have tried to follow the evidence wherever it would lead. If the reader finds a personal hero or two entangled in New Age concepts, this should not be taken as a personal judgment of those individuals. Rather, it is an indication of how far this influence has spread and has been taken into the daily life of the Church. I can only hope that truth has not been sustained at the expense of charity.

In attempting to discern errors, one runs—of course—the risk of finding them, and in finding and exposing them one commits the supreme "sin" of intolerance. Western culture, which can seemingly stomach any perversity, is quite intolerant about one thing: intolerance. We live in a society that values, perhaps above all, tolerance. Tolerance of other viewpoints, especially religious viewpoints, is demanded.

The reason for such tolerance lies not with any truth inherent in opposite viewpoints. Such a notion would be absurd, as two contradictory beliefs cannot both be true. But tolerance is often the best course to take—not because men are wise and good, but because men are often evil and cannot be trusted to deal justly with their fellowman. For this reason, a large measure of tolerance is a virtue in this world.

Within the Church, however, there must be limits beyond which the title "Christian" can no longer apply. The Church is not wedded to the passions of the moment, but bound to the truth without regard for any momentary twists currently popular with those individuals who are given over to the latest scientific or philosophic musings. This "dogmatic relativism" was rejected by Pope Pius XII in the Encyclical *Humani Generis*. He wrote that the way in which we express the truth:

> is capable of being perfected and polished; and we know also that the Church itself has not always used the same terms in the same way. [But] it is also manifest that the Church cannot be bound to every system of philosophy that has existed for a short space of time.
>
> This is supreme impudence and something that would make dogma itself a reed shaken by the wind.[1]

The Apostle Peter was neither sparing nor gentle in his condemnations. He warned the faithful:

> But there were also false prophets among the people, even as there shall be among you lying teachers, who shall bring in sects of perdition, and deny the Lord who bought them: bringing upon themselves swift destruction . . .
>
> For it had been better for them not to have known the way of justice, than after they have known it, to turn back from that holy commandment which was delivered to them. (*2 Ptr.* 2:1,21).

---

1. Pius XII, *Humani Generis* (Boston: Daughters of St. Paul, 1950), pp. 16-17.

Scripture is clear in its treatment of those who steadfastly bring shame on the body of Christ. St. Paul brooks no compromise in his *First Letter to the Corinthians:*

> I wrote to you in an epistle, not to keep company with fornicators. I mean not with the fornicators of this world, or with the covetous, or the extortioners, or the servers of idols; otherwise you must needs go out of this world. But now I have written to you, not to keep company, if any man that is named a brother, be a fornicator, or covetous, or a server of idols, or a railer, or a drunkard, or an extortioner: with such a one, not so much as to eat. For what have I to do to judge them that are without? Do not you judge them that are within? For them that are without, God will judge. Put away the evil one from among yourselves. (*1 Cor.* 5:9-13).

This, then, is the basis of my "intolerance." Criticism is easy and I will, as much as possible, try to let individuals speak for themselves. The purpose is not to condemn the individuals involved, but to permit the reader to understand these errors and the forces behind them. God knows fully what motives lie behind words and actions, and He will judge correctly. Nevertheless, it is every Catholic's duty to judge teachings and actions in light of the truth he claims to hold and serve. This book, then, is an effort at sound judgment in the light of truth.

—RANDY ENGLAND

Introduction:

Change. . .or Exchange?

*"Who changed the truth of God into a lie;
and worshipped and served the creature
rather than the Creator. . ."*
(Rom. 1:25).

What is happening in the Church today? Are the changes
we have experienced in the more than twenty years since Vatican II nothing more than the Catholic Church's entry into the
modern age? For myself, I could understand the use of the
vernacular at Mass, but some people are still uncomfortable
with it. Other changes in liturgy and devotion have been
widely accepted. Still, many Catholics find them distasteful.
Unfortunately, those faithful who are not comfortable with
change are subtly ridiculed as reactionaries or worse. But who
has not been uncomfortable with certain of the following
novelties?

Novelties such as:

- A separate "feminist spirituality" for women that
  goes "beyond God the Father" and instead
  celebrates self and seeks to connect with nature
  or "the Goddess." Such a system demands a
  matriarchal society and cannot accept a male God
  or Saviour.

- A new "mission" for missionaries which does not include any motive of conversion to the Catholic Religion. Missionaries who seek "wisdom" at the feet of Hindu holy men and whose writings quote from the Hindu and Chinese scriptures with more awe and reverence than they accord the Bible.

- Catholic priests who run Hindu ashrams disguised as Catholic "retreat houses," and Catholic bishops who support them.

- "New Age" Catholic schools that are chiefly interested in teaching values for an un-Christian one-world government and the coming New Age. Such basic items as the Ten Commandments and belief in the Resurrection are considered dispensable.

- A Jesuit from India who has taught Eastern meditation to Catholic clergy and laity alike. His techniques bring the "seeker" into contact with demons visualized as wise spirit guides.

- An extremely popular Dominican priest who maintains that the practice of traditional Christianity is equivalent to "whoring after past gods." In the New Age, we are to worship the creation...and the creature.

- Courses, tapes and books that promise to "teach us how to pray." These new prayers, billed as ancient Christian techniques, turn out to be doorways to altered states of consciousness and demonic realms.

- The rehabilitation of the condemned teachings of Jesuit Pierre Teilhard de Chardin. Teilhard is the premier inspiration for New Agers, both Catholic and non-Catholic alike.

- A Catholic theologian who accepts the possibility of reincarnation and that God will ultimately relent and allow all men into Heaven. He expects that shamanism (witchcraft) will become the norm as we move into a New Age of global consciousness.

- A Franciscan priest who travels the circuit of Catholic churches and convents teaching the faithful how to manipulate reality with their minds, using the aid and counsel of spirit beings.

- Numerous large national Catholic publishers who peddle books and tapes which include yoga, mantra chanting, New Age music, healing meditations, Eastern religions and Intensive Journaling through occult meditation. These are all presented as avenues to enhanced Catholic "spirituality."

These examples are of a completely different order from the external changes the Church has experienced. For here we are dealing with such issues as the Deity of Jesus Christ and the Way of salvation.

Unfortunately, change, even needed change, has long coattails. The often-cited "Spirit of Vatican II" has too often been ample excuse for innovators to experiment with a faith which, for them, has lost its meaning. Their beliefs are often part of what is known as the New Age Movement. This book will show how its pagan philosophy has infiltrated the life and institutions of the Catholic Church.

St. John the Apostle, when an old man exiled on the Aegean island of Patmos for proclaiming the word of God, received an appropriate message from Our Lord and addressed it to a church that had a fine reputation in the world. The message was simple: "Be watchful, and strengthen the things that remain, which are ready to die." (*Apoc.* 3:2).

The Church has survived two thousand years, much of that time under attack. Yet, in the last one hundred years, the breeze has stiffened; there is a malignancy in the air—the breath of the Evil One. True, man is capable of much mischief, but the New Age Movement is not from men. It is from hostile, superintelligent beings masquerading as angels of light. Their appeal is to brotherhood and peace for a miserable world—a world ripe for harvest and judgment.

1.

The New Age Movement

*"The soul goes round upon a wheel of stars and all
things return....Good and evil go round in a wheel
that is one thing and not many. Do you not realize
in your heart, do you not believe behind all your
beliefs, that there is but one reality and we are its
shadows; and that all things are but aspects of one
thing; a center where men melt into Man and Man
into God?"*

"No," said Father Brown.
   —G. K. Chesterton, *The Dagger with Wings*

Ideally, I would launch immediately into my subject, but
the matter requires a familiarity with the material and its history. Readers already familiar with the background of the New
Age Movement may wish to skim this chapter.

The New Age Movement is a worldwide phenomenon osten-
sibly dedicated to the ideas of the interconnectedness of all
things and the powers of the human mind. In the New Age,
knowledge supersedes faith and heralds a break with Western
values and thought. Its goals are a one-world government, a
one-world religion, and a one-world christ. These are not
necessarily bad, not necessarily un-Christian. The question is:
Which christ? Which religion?

Regarding a one-world government, the Bible seems to

show that a united mankind—united not under God, but under man's own flag—is not a good thing. It has been tried before. At the Tower of Babel, God had to intervene in order to put down man's arrogant effort to set himself up as his own god. God knew the evil result and prevented our unification. Confusing the language and scattering mankind throughout the earth, God graciously kept us from our own pride. (*Gen.* 11:9).

We need only to look around at how some nations now oppress and even murder their own citizens. At least they are restrained in part by the disapproval of other nations and in greater part by their own borders. What will the torturers do when they know neither borders nor disapproving onlookers? Apart from grace, fallen man cannot live as one. The fantasy must wait.

St. Paul writes unequivocally that a new world leader will appear before the Second Coming of Christ. The Apostle tells of a great falling away from the Church and the rise of the Anti-Christ or "man of sin":

> Let no man deceive you by any means, for unless there come a revolt first, and the man of sin be revealed, the son of perdition, who opposeth, and is lifted up above all that is called God, or that is worshipped, so that he sitteth in the temple of God, shewing himself as if he were God. Remember you not, that when I was yet with you, I told you these things? And now you know what withholdeth, that he may be revealed in his time. For the mystery of iniquity already worketh; only that he who now holdeth, do hold, until he be taken out of the way. And then that wicked one shall be revealed whom the Lord Jesus shall kill with the spirit of his mouth; and shall destroy with the brightness of his coming, him, whose coming is according to the working of Satan, in all power, and signs, and lying wonders, and in all seduction of iniquity to them that perish; because they receive not the love of the truth, that they might be saved. Therefore God shall send them the operation of error, to

believe lying: that all may be judged who have not
believed the truth, but have consented to iniquity. (*2
Thess.* 2:3-11).

The *Didache,* or "Teachings of the Twelve Apostles," which
is one of the earliest extra-biblical Christian documents,
teaches: "For in the last days...the Deceiver of the world will
appear, claiming to be the Son of God, and giving striking
exhibitions of power; the earth will be given over to his
hands...." (*Didache* 16:4).[1]

The "withholder" or "restrainer" referred to by St. Paul has
variously been explained as St. Michael the Archangel, the
Mass, the presence of the Church or the Holy Spirit. This
"restrainer" of the Anti-Christ may be removed directly by
God, or the indicated removal may reflect the loss of the
influence of the Church or Holy Spirit as a result of the
apostasy.

We wonder, as did Jesus' disciples: "...when shall these
things be?" And Jesus tells us: "But of that day and hour no
one knoweth, no not the angels of heaven, but the Father
alone." (*Matt.* 24:3,36). What is certain is that the day will
come, and when it does come it may be the New Age Movement which fosters the apostasy; this Movement may be the
very delusion which will prepare the world for the
Anti-Christ.

The New Age Movement is as old as mankind, and although
its beliefs have probably never been without adherents, it needs
no human continuity to maintain its ancient tenets, for all its
essential elements flow straight from Hell. The first victims
of the New Age Movement are well-known. In fact, we have
all inherited an attraction for its lies: And the woman answered
him (the serpent), saying:

---

1. James A. Kleist, S.J., Ph.D. (translator), *Ancient Christian Writers: The
Works of the Fathers in Translation* (Westminster, Maryland: Newman
Press, 1948), p. 24.

Of the fruit of the trees that are in paradise we do eat;
but of the fruit of the tree which is in the midst of paradise, God hath commanded us that we should not eat;
and that we should not touch it, lest perhaps we die. And
the serpent said to the woman: No, you shall not die
the death. For God doth know that in what day soever
you shall eat thereof, your eyes shall be opened: and you
shall be as Gods, knowing good and evil. (*Gen.* 3:2-5).

These two lies are the foundation of every pagan religion
and cult:

- You will not die.
- You will be like God.

In every imaginable fashion these ideas are woven into endless
patterns, along with enough truth to fool nearly anyone. They
are found in the doctrines of reincarnation and the divinity
of man. In the New Age, the wages of sin is not death, but
just another go around in another life. Nothing really matters.
There is no personal Creator-God to interfere with the attrac-
tions of pride and sensuality—no one to whom we must give
account. And even if God did exist, what claim could He
make upon us, His fellow gods?

Modernism, Immanence and Pantheism

The supposedly Catholic equivalent of the New Age Movement began to exert a strong influence in the seminaries of
the Church before the turn of the century. Strangely enough,
this old heresy was called by the name of "Modernism." Pope
St. Pius X, in his encyclical *Pascendi (Dominici) Gregis* or
On the Doctrines of the Modernists, undertook a description
of the problem, realizing how obscure, shadowy and uncon-
nected all the threads seemed. Nevertheless, he boldly traced
the connections and exposed Modernism, beginning a period
of purification in the Church that unfortunately died soon after
him. From the encyclical, *Pascendi:*

> We must now interrupt a silence, which it would be
> criminal to prolong, that we may point out to the whole
> Church, as they really are, men who are badly
> disguised.
>
> It is one of the cleverest devices of the Modern-
> ists...to present their doctrines without order and sys-
> tematic arrangement, in a scattered and disjointed
> manner so as to make it appear as if their minds were
> in doubt or hesitation, whereas in reality they are quite
> firm and steadfast. For this reason it will be of advan-
> tage to bring their teachings together here into one
> group, and to point out their interconnection....²

Christians have always worshipped the God who created
the universe. He made it from nothing and is distinct from
it. "Thou hast created all things; and for thy will they were,
and have been created." (*Apoc.* 4:11).

The doctrine of immanence is the idea that God is not separate and distinct from His creation, but that He is (somehow)
diffused throughout it while at the same time the creation
is (somehow) diffused throughout God. And yet the Church
has always taught a similar idea: that God is omnipresent.
This is clear from Scripture, as King David wrote:

> Whither shall I go from thy spirit? or whither shall
> I flee from thy face? If I ascend into heaven, thou art
> there: if I descend into hell, thou art present. If I take
> my wings early in the morning, and dwell in the utter-
> most parts of the sea: Even there also shall thy hand lead
> me: and thy right hand shall hold me. (*Ps.* 138:7-10).

Apart from this natural omnipresence, there is also the
supernatural presence of God through His grace. Truly, every
member of Christ's Church who is in the state of grace is
indwelt by the Holy Spirit, but neither is this what is meant
by immanence.

---

2. Pope St. Pius X, *Pascendi Gregis* (London: Burns & Oates, Ltd.,
1907), p. 56. (Reprinted by Neumann Press, Long Prairie, MN.)

Proponents of this sort of "immanence" believe either that there is no God out there at all, or that if He is out there, then He is unknowable. In practice, this means that man must not look outward to a God separate from himself, but rather to the god within. We must look inside ourselves if we will learn of God. In fact, the Modernist New Age perspective considers the concept of a God outside ourselves to be absurd and even revolting. The key is to go within. Pius X understood the distinction when he wrote: "Religion. . .must, like every other fact, admit of some explanation. [When] all external revelation [is] absolutely denied, it is clear that this explanation will be sought in vain outside of man himself. It must, therefore, be looked for in man."[3]

As St. Pius X was producing his encyclical, G.K. Chesterton was writing his classic work, *Orthodoxy*. In it, he spoke of the insufficiency of the "Inner Light":

> Of all the conceivable forms of enlightenment the worst is what these people call the Inner Light. Of all horrible religions the most horrible is the worship of the god within. Any one who knows any body (sic) knows how it would work. . . .That Jones shall worship the god within him turns out ultimately to mean that Jones shall worship Jones. Let Jones worship the sun or moon, anything rather than the Inner Light; let Jones worship cats or crocodiles, if he can find any in his street, but not the god within. Christianity came into the world firstly in order to assert with violence that a man had not only to look inwards, but to look outwards, to behold with astonishment and enthusiasm a divine company and a divine captain. The only fun of being a Christian was that a man was not left alone with the Inner Light, but definitely recognized an outer light, fair as the sun, clear as the moon, terrible as an army with banners. . . .
>
> That transcendence and distinctness of the deity which some Christians now want to remove from

---

3. *Ibid.*, p. 8.

Christianity, was really the only reason any one wanted to be a Christian.[4]

Pius X taught that the Modernists' (and I would add the New Agers') concept of "god immanent" squares best with Pantheism. He asked, "Does or does not this 'Immanence' leave God distinct from man? If it does not, it is Pantheism."[5]

Pantheism simply means that God is Everything and that Everything is God. Pantheism is the natural upshot of the doctrine of immanence, though many Catholic New Agers (forgive the oxymoron) try to draw convoluted arguments to the contrary. One popular writer-speaker-Dominican priest has tried to sidestep the charge of heresy by calling the doctrine of God immanent "pan*en*theism," or as he explains it: "God is in everything, and everything is in God."[6]

With just a little verbal shuffling, the lie is obscured and made palatable. The phrase may not be instantly recognized as false, but something is wrong. Often, the New Ager will use innocent-sounding language, but with a new and different twist. In this example the writer uses his "panentheism" as a starting point from which he develops what eventually turns out to be open paganism and witchcraft—but more on that later.

No matter what you call it, pantheism dilutes the idea of God so thoroughly that in the end all meaning disappears. In J.D. Salinger's story, "Teddy," a ten-year-old boy recounts his realization of the pantheistic god: "I was six when I saw that everything was God...It was on a Sunday, I remember. My sister was...drinking her milk and all of a sudden I saw that she was God and the milk was God. I mean all she was doing was pouring God into God, if you know what I mean."[7]

4. G.K. Chesterton, *Orthodoxy* (Garden City, NY: Doubleday Image, 1959), pp. 76-78.
5. Pius X, *Pascendi,* pp. 23, 50.
6. Matthew Fox, *Original Blessing* (Santa Fe, NM: Bear & Company, 1983), p. 90.
7. J.D. Salinger, *Nine Stories* (Boston: Little, Brown and Company, 1953), p. 288.

Holism and Hinduism

Holism (Wholism) is the view that all things are interconnected and form a single entity. This entity or "whole" has an independent reality which is greater than the sum of its parts. This is the viewpoint of Hinduism and has its foundation in the experience of the individual.

In Christianity, our leaders are those who, through their faith and obedience to God, teach us about Him. Some of our earliest teachers were directly inspired by God to write the Bible. The Hindu teacher, or guru, should not be seen in the same way, but rather as a tour guide.

It is as if, when St. John on Patmos had received the Revelation (*Apocalypse*), rather than writing down the revealed truth, he had opened a school instructing aspiring Christians in his methods for corresponding with God. He would insist that the truth was impossible to communicate. John's advice would be for the Christian to find his own connection with the source. That is the advice now popular with many Catholic teachers today.

It is the task of the guru to teach methods, not doctrine. The aim is to achieve an altered state of consciousness during which the seeker experiences the "oneness" of all things.

In the West we see one thing as being distinct from another. If I say, "This is a chair and this is a dog and this is my foot," anyone listening would understand. The Hindu or Buddhist would maintain that these things are not at all distinct from one another. Instead, it is I that have arbitrarily imposed my view of reality.

More to the point, these particulars have no reality at all. They are illusion. The only reality is that of the mind; the only purpose: to achieve a oneness with the universal mind. We are to get past the logical view and "realize" that there is no separation between the self and all others. The guru's job is to show the way.

The fact that the individual must experience for himself this ultimate does not mean there is no actual doctrine. The "truths" experienced can be expressed in words, but cannot actually be "known" without the experience. This is not a religion of faith and reason, but of experiential knowledge. The belief system generated through altered states of consciousness is strikingly similar from one individual to the next. The distance between experiences may be a thousand miles or a thousand years, but the message is the same. This remarkable (though not perfect) agreement is considered by many as a proof of truth. What it most probably suggests, however, is not truth, but a common source. What follow are a number of these common New Age practices and techniques, as well as many of the beliefs which seem to flow from them.

Reincarnation

Reincarnationists believe that individual souls are recycled over and over again in new human or animal bodies. Each person's present station in life, whether privileged or poverty-stricken, results from his actions in former lives (which has formed his Karma). For reincarnationists, "Salvation" means to escape the laws of Rebirth and of Karma by uniting oneself with (losing oneself in) the absolute, but for most souls the future seems to hold only more cycles. It is difficult to see the appeal in these usually endless, dizzying cycles, especially when the alternative is as straightforward as following Christ, with His promise of eternal happiness. But reincarnation is a theory that has the appearance of getting around the fact of death and judgment.

A "Catholic" theologian has written a book attempting to reconcile Christian belief with psychic phenomena. He counsels against rejecting the doctrine of reincarnation outright, even though Scripture certainly does reject it. And he considers reincarnation the most plausible explanation for certain cases.[8]

---

8. John J. Heaney, *The Sacred and the Psychic: Parapsychology & Christian Theology* (New York: Paulist Press, 1984), p. 211.

Unfortunately, there are too many such Christians who examine the issue of reincarnation superficially. Certain strange cases seem to them most easily explained by invoking the doctrine of reincarnation. Others seize upon certain Bible verses, taken out of context, to support the concept.

A passage that the reincarnationists like to point to is *Matthew* 11:13-14. Jesus is speaking of the role of St. John the Baptist: "For all the prophets and the law prophesied until John. And if you will receive it, he is Elias that is to come."

Does this mean that John was Elias reincarnated? No, what the angel told Zachary in the Temple was that his son John would go before the Lord "in the spirit and power of Elias" (*Luke* 1:17). To go "in the spirit and power of Elias" is certainly different from being Elias and is not without precedent. Eliseus' last request before Elias was taken into heaven was that he would receive a double portion of Elias' spirit. (*4 Kgs.* 2:9). No one suggests that Eliseus was Elias reincarnated. When the priests asked St. John the Baptist: "Art thou Elias?" he said, "I am not." (*John* 1:21).

Defenders of reincarnation also quote Our Lord's saying, "I lay down my life, that I may take it again. No man taketh it away from me: but I lay it down of myself, and I have power to lay it down: and I have power to take it up again." (*John* 10:17-18). To infer reincarnation from this statement would obviously require sweeping aside Our Lord's clear meaning, as well as the historical fact of His Resurrection with the same body and same soul. As He said to the Apostles after His Resurrection: "...it is I, fear not....See my hands and feet, that it is I myself..." (*Luke* 24:36, 39). "And if Christ be not risen again, your faith is vain, for you are yet in your sins...But now Christ is risen from the dead..." (*1 Cor.* 15:17, 20).

The most familiar "proofs" for reincarnation come from persons who have been hypnotically "regressed" in order to experience supposed past lives. While many such regressions can be dismissed as works of fraudulent showmanship, there are cases concerning persons who describe places where they have never been, or speak languages they have never learned. Some such cases may be explained by the fact that the hypnotist activates long-forgotten memories, perhaps from earliest childhood. More ominous still is the possibility that the subject, in a trance state, is made vulnerable to the influence of demonic spirits. In this event, there is virtually no limit to the wealth of accurate and verifiable "proofs" which might be provided by the spirits in order to convince those eager to be so deceived.

Considered even more convincing are cases in which a young child is believed to recall its previous life. In the typical case, researchers do not arrive on the scene until after the child's recollections have solidified. These children, many from cultures accustomed to the idea of reincarnation, naturally are highly suggestible and subject to the coaching of their elders. Such proofs are thought to be strengthened when the child possesses a deformity or birthmark supposedly relating to the manner of death previously endured. Proponents surmise that the "memory" of dismemberment in a previous life is supported by the fact that a limb is missing in the present life. Reason might offer an alternate explanation. Perhaps it is the missing limb which gives rise to so-called "recollection" of the previous life.

Another theory is that a child's (or adult's) phobias are holdovers from an earlier life. For example, a fear of guns means that a person was previously shot to death. Also, child prodigies who manifest precocious talents in music, art or sports are said to be the reincarnations of gifted deceased persons. These arguments have the same merit as the birthmark cases. Indeed, Junior's artistic scribbling might cause speculation that he is Michelangelo reborn. So what?

However little or much these cases may seem to prove, it is important to examine what the Church and Scripture say. Where do souls come from if they are not pre-existent, as reincarnationists believe?

In the encyclical *Humani Generis,* Pope Pius XII taught that "souls are immediately created by God." From Scripture we learn that souls have never lived before. In *Romans* 9:11, St. Paul refers to Jacob and Esau "when the children were not yet born, nor had done any good or evil." Clearly, had they lived before, no one could assert that the brothers had done neither good nor evil.

We also know that the soul has a destination immediately upon death. As Dr. Ludwig Ott summarizes it in his benchmark work, *Fundamentals of Catholic Dogma*, Pope Benedict XII, in the dogmatic constitution *Benedictus Deus* (1336), taught that the souls of the Just that are completely pure enter Heaven immediately after death, and the souls of the other Just enter Heaven after their purification (in Purgatory). They become partakers in the vision of the Divine Essence, and are truly blessed, while the souls of those in mortal sin immediately enter Hell, and are subject to the torments of Hell. (D. 530 f.).[9]

Moreover, Scripture tells us: "It is appointed unto men once to die, and after this the judgment." (*Heb.* 9:27). The Scriptural story of Lazarus and Dives (the rich man) shows these men immediately after death going to "the bosom of Abraham" and to Hell, respectively. (*Luke* 16:22). In *Luke* 23:43 Our Lord certainly gives the Good Thief no time for reincarnation when He says to him, "This day thou shalt be with me in paradise." Our Lord said of Judas that it would have been better for him if he had not been born. (*Matt.* 26:24). Would He have said this if the tragic Apostle were going to have another life in which to improve his "Karma"? And the Old Testament book of *Ecclesiasticus* speaks of blessedness "in the day of death": "With him that feareth the Lord, it shall go well in the latter end, and in the day of his death he shall be blessed." (*Ecclus.* 1:13).

The Apostles' Creed declares, "I believe in. . .the resurrection of the body, and life everlasting." Neither does Scripture

---

9. Dr. Ludwig Ott, *Fundamentals of Catholic Dogma* (Cork: Mercier Press, 1955; Rockford, IL: TAN Books and Publishers, Inc., 1974), p. 475.

leave open any provision for reincarnation at a later time. Instead, resurrection and final judgment will occur after the Second Coming of Christ. Jesus Himself warned: "For the hour cometh, wherein all that are in the graves shall hear the voice of the Son of God. And they that have done good things, shall come forth unto the resurrection of life; but they that have done evil, unto the resurrection of judgment." (*John* 5:28-29).

Moreover, the Church teaches *de fide* that the dead will rise again with the same bodies as they had on earth: "They will arise with their bodies which they have now." (D. 429). This proclamation was made at the Fourth Lateran Council in the year 1215.[10]

There is no way a Catholic Christian can believe in reincarnation. To do so means to go against both Scripture and the teachings of the Church. It stretches reason. A decision must be made between two absolutely incompatible alternatives: Reincarnation and Resurrection.

The Divinity of Man

When the individual "realizes" his oneness with everything and his oneness with God, it follows that he is a full partner in that divinity. This should not be taken in just a philosophic sense. If one is a god, he ought to be in control of the universe. Through the occult technique of visualization, the practitioner believes that he does in fact create his own universe, continuously. Imagine having such power! Imagine using it! That is exactly what the New Agers would have us do.

Even the business world is learning the value of false pride as a motivator and the benefits of using altered states of consciousness as a "technology" for creating change. Companies as diverse as Pacific Bell, Proctor & Gamble, TRW, Ford Motor Company and Polaroid have signed up New Age consultants or started up training courses in New Age thinking. In the

---

10. Ott, p. 490.

forefront has been Werner Erhard—of *est* (Erhard Seminar Training) fame—who has founded Transformational Technologies, "a business designed to do for companies what *est* did for individuals." Transtech fees totaled $15 million in 1986.[11]

New Age training techniques are very appealing to corporate managers because they bypass the employee's reasoning faculties by means of the meditative state. These techniques—self-hypnosis, meditation, centering, visualization, guided imagery and yoga—facilitate the goal of the training, which is to get everyone thinking alike (called "getting aligned"). It sounds good if you do not mind letting someone else think for you. It sounds good unless you object to having yourself initiated into the whole demonic New Age system.

More than one rebellious employee has allegedly been fired for his refusal to participate in New Age training programs, and a number have been to the courts for relief. Pacific Bell was immersed in controversy in 1987 as the California Public Utilities Commission undertook an investigation of its New Age training program called "Kroning."[12]

In the high-pressure, high-stress business world, well-meaning managers are always looking for ways to become more effective. Superiors or co-workers are always pushing numerous different "tape series" or books for self-improvement.

One of the earliest and most influential of the success motivation/positive mental attitude gurus was Napoleon Hill. His book, *Think and Grow Rich,* is a staple in the business world. In it he teaches the sorcerer's techniques of meditation and visualization to create wealth and success. In Hill's lesser-known book, *Grow Rich With Peace of Mind,* he explains that these techniques were revealed to him by disembodied Ascended Masters. He writes:

Now and again I have had evidence that unseen

---

11. Annette Miller, "Corporate Mind Control," *Newsweek,* 4 May 1987, pp. 38-39.
12. *Ibid.*

friends hover about me, unknowable to the ordinary senses. In my studies I discovered there is a group of strange beings who maintain a school of wisdom. . . .

The School has Masters who can disembody themselves and travel instantly to any place they choose. . .to give knowledge directly, by voice. . . .

Now I knew that one of these masters had come across thousands of miles, through the night, into my study. . . .

I shall not set down every word he said. . .much of what he said already has been presented to you in the chapters of this book and will follow in other chapters.

"You have earned the right to reveal a Supreme Secret to others," said the vibrant voice. "You have been under the guidance of the Great School. . . . Now you must give the world a blueprint. . . ."[13]

This "blueprint" is echoed by the formula around which all the business success/motivation materials revolve. These materials are so much like one another that a single description would cover most that have ever been produced.

It was shortly after I had become aware of the New Age Movement that I began to look into some of the so-called "success" tapes that I had been listening to. One day, I happened to be traveling with my boss when he brought up the subject of an upcoming promotion review panel which one of my managers would be attending. It would, of course, be very important for the manager to present himself well if he were to be selected for promotion. The boss handed me a book (the name of which I have since forgotten).

"Here is a book I'd like you to give to Dennis to read before the promotion review board. I read it right before I faced the board, and it works!"

I began to flip through the pages. The introduction promised a changed life if only I would follow the principles revealed

---

13. Napoleon Hill, *Grow Rich With Peace of Mind* (New York: Ballantine Books, 1967), pp. 158-160 (as quoted by Dave Hunt, *The Seduction of Christianity,* pp. 18-19).

in the following pages. Chapter Two got down to business as it began with the concepts of self-hypnosis and visualization. I shut the book to play a game with the boss. I said:

"I've never seen this book before, but I'll tell you what it says. I'll bet it starts with special relaxation exercises where you begin either lying down or sitting erect in a chair and begin to imagine each part of the body as it becomes totally relaxed."

"That's right!" he said.

"Next," I went on, "it tells you to imagine, to picture in your mind, yourself in that particular situation in which you want to find yourself. If you want to be rich, see a picture of yourself as rich. If you want power and success, see yourself as successful and powerful. Visualize the new car that you want. Whatever it is, visualize it as if it was already yours, believe it, and do it daily. You will bring it about through the power of your mind."

He was shocked. "How did you know?"

"Let me finish," I said with a pride I ought not to have had. "Finally, somewhere in here it says that you are in absolute, complete control of your life and everything connected with it. In effect, it says that you are God."

At this point he nearly drove off the road as he reached for the book to show me the last chapter. I read the page where he directed me. It said that I was now ready for the real secret. I read the words: YOU ARE GOD! Now even I was a little unnerved, as my game was more on target than I had imagined. I told him that I was a Catholic and if I were to recommend the practice of Catholicism as a means to prepare for a review board, I would probably be called down for it. The contents of his book were just as much a religion as mine, only this was an amalgam of Eastern mysticism, voodoo and witchcraft.

He protested that it works and that it really gave him the confidence to win out at his promotion review. I agreed with him, because, after all, one ought to be completely confident if he believes he is a god. But what will happen when that first inevitable failure occurs, and the whole fragile fraud comes down? If one is a Christian he is confident not because of personal greatness, but because "I can do all things in him who strengtheneth me." (*Phil.* 4:13).

My boss was quiet for awhile and then took back the book, saying that he could see now that he should never have shown it to me. Our conversation turned to another subject.

The divinity of man was the key idea taught in Werner Erhard's *est*. John Denver, graduate of *est* and follower of the Swami Muktananda, said of his two mentors: "They're running the universe. They're gods and they know it."[14] About his own future, Denver said: "I can do anything. One of these days I'll be so complete I won't be a human. I'll be a god."[15]

The guru is worshipped as a god by his followers, and he thrives on it. The pleasures of pride are as irresistible to him as they were to his father, the devil:

> How art thou fallen from heaven, O Lucifer, who didst rise in the morning?...And thou saidst in thy heart:
> "I will ascend into heaven,
> "I will exalt my throne above the stars of God,
> "I will sit in the mountain of the covenant...
> "I will ascend above the height of the clouds,
> "I will be like the most High."
> But yet thou shalt be brought down to hell, into the depth of the pit. (*Isaias* 14:12-14)

C.S. Lewis called Pride the great sin: "According to Christian teachers, the essential vice, the utmost evil, is Pride. ...it was through Pride that the devil became the devil: Pride leads to every other vice: it is the complete anti-God state of mind."[16]

---

14. Maureen Orth, *Newsweek*, 20 Dec. 1976, p. 66.
15. *Ibid.,* p. 68.
16. C.S. Lewis, *Mere Christianity* (New York: Macmillan, 1979), p. 94.

Pride is the greatest of the seven capital sins. According to Scripture, ". . . pride is the beginning of all sin: he that holdeth it, shall be filled with maledictions, and it shall ruin him in the end." (*Ecclus.* 10:15). The book of *Tobias* (4:14) puts it this way: "Never suffer pride to reign in thy mind, or in thy words: for from it all perdition took its beginning."

One day, I was tuned into a Christian radio station. My ears perked up as the speaker assured me: "It doesn't matter who you are, Christian or not, nothing is a greater barrier to happiness today than low self-esteem."

"Really?" I thought, "Nothing is a greater barrier? Not even the fact that one is lost?"

The lady preacher continued on, bludgeoning the beast of low self-esteem with the club of human pride. Although appeals to pride would normally seem most shocking coming over a Christian radio station, this no longer seems at all incongruous in light of today's human potential movement.

There is scarcely a more universally accepted maxim in today's culture than that most individuals' unhappiness and psychological problems stem from low self-esteem. Just as well-accepted is the supposed cure for the problem: Build up that low self-esteem. They say that children (and adults) need acceptance, achievement, success, and so on. Since we have no lack of good advice and psychological opinion, the list is long. Is meeting the demands of such a laundry list the solution to the problem of low self-esteem?

First of all: What is low self-esteem? Certainly it is not a failure to love oneself. The biblical command to love your neighbor as yourself clearly implies that our love of self is a given. Even common sense should tell us that we love ourselves already. As Dave Hunt (a Protestant writer on the New Age) notes:

> Of course, there are many who express varying degrees of self-hatred. That they don't actually hate themselves can easily be seen. The person who says, "I'm so ugly, I hate myself!" doesn't hate himself at all, or he would

be glad that he was ugly. It is because he loves himself
that he is upset with his appearance and the way people
respond to him. The person who grovels in depression
and says he hates himself for having wasted his life
would actually be glad that he had wasted his life if he
really hated himself. In fact, he is unhappy about having
wasted his life because he loves himself.[17]

How *should* we see ourselves? An exalted view of oneself
is not the answer, for that is the foulest sin of all. A prideful
person forgets or denies that he is a creature, that everything
he has is from God, and that God keeps him in existence
from minute to minute. Then again, low self-esteem is certainly a miserable state, itself created by human pride which
has been twisted and tormented by personal failure and the
want of love. What then? Many would say one should have
a "healthy self-respect." That is good. But it does not move
us toward knowing what a "healthy self-respect" is, nor does
it tell us how to get there.

Again, let us hear Dave Hunt on the proper status of the
self:

> The Bible says that we were created in the image of
> God (*Genesis* 1:26). What do you think of when you
> think of an image? The first thing you think of is a mir-
> ror. A mirror has one purpose and one purpose only
> and that is to reflect an image other than its own....
> Now what would you think of a mirror that tries to
> develop a good self-image? ...We got problems, folks.
> If there is something wrong with the image in the mir-
> ror, what the mirror needs to do is get back in the right
> relationship with the One whose image it was designed
> to reflect. But instead of that we're being turned to self,
> instead of to Him. Self-confidence, Self development,
> Self improvement...Self *ad nauseam.*
>
> A young person who gets up in a high school speech

---

17. Dave Hunt, *The Seduction of Christianity: Spiritual Discernment in the Last Days* (Eugene, OR: Harvest House Publishers, 1985), p. 199.

class and his kness knock and he stutters and he can't say what he's trying to say. . .what did we call that person? Self-conscious, right? What's that person's problem? They're thinking of themselves.[18]

The cure for low self-esteem is not to build up one's pride. The remedy is the same as for high self-esteem, that is, no self-esteem, or "forgetfulness of self," as it is described in lives of the saints. Why be dwelling on the self at all? When the relationship with God is right, all other relationships—including with oneself—are right. It is that condition which gives perfect assurance, yet "in humility, let each esteem others better than themselves. . ." (*Phil.* 2:3).

Contrast this with the New Age goal to become gods ourselves. Many are already convinced. They believe that eventually everyone will be. Meanwhile, they work and wait and meditate, confident that the dawn will yet come for most of the rest of us.

Evolution

Darwin was not the first to teach the theory of evolution. This ancient belief is an absolute article of faith and central to New Age-Modernist thought—and not only in the biological sphere. According to the New Age, man is perfectible, and divinity is our collective destiny. We are supposedly moving toward what the Jesuit priest, Pierre Teilhard de Chardin, called the Omega Point. In his view, matter has struggled throughout the millennia, becoming increasingly complex, ultimately giving birth to humankind. Only the final step awaits us as we are lured on toward unity with "OMEGA," or God.

The view of the Catholic Church on biological evolution has been cautious. In *Humani Generis,* Pius XII permitted discussion of evolution by competent thinkers, but warned

---

18. Talk by Dave Hunt, Counter Cult Conference, May 26, 1984.

against any presumption that evolution had been proved true,
"as if there were nothing in the sources of Divine Revelation
which demands the greatest moderation and caution in this
question."[19] Pius XII's caution was justified; since his death
the theory has had some resounding problems.

Despite evolution's scientific mantle or the latest court decision, the theory is proving increasingly faulty with each passing decade. In light of the New Agers' preoccupation with
personal experience, evolution may be the only belief that
New Agers take on faith. And it must be taken on faith,
because it has never been observed to occur, and the scientific
evidence needed to support it does not exist.

When Darwin's *Origin of Species* was published in 1859,
paleontology was in its infancy, the fossil record as yet unex-
plored. The years have been cruel to the theory of gradual
evolution. The process of natural selection requires a slow,
progressive period of development, a period during which the
evolving organism, throughout successive generations, grows
legs or wings or whatever.

There are two problems here. One is that the fossil record
shows no gradual development from lower organisms to
higher. Rather, it shows that species remain generally
unchanged throughout time. Those represented in the most
ancient fossils are basically indistinguishable from their
descendants living today. The fossil record shows creatures
that suddenly appear in the world, without apparent ances-
tors. Some become extinct, while others survive unchanged.
The theory demands that there should be transitional forms
between evolutionary developments, some sort of creature
destined to become a bird whose forepaws are halfway
toward becoming wings. Yet, evidence of such transitional
forms is missing, hence the term "missing links." (This leads
to the question how one can build a theory around evidence
that is "missing," but apparently that is only a minor

---

19. Pius XII, *Humani Generis*, p. 36.

difficulty for evolutionists.)

The second problem is the supposed mechanism by which evolution is powered. Mutations (which do occur, but are nearly always detrimental) cause changes in the organism, and those which are favorable are retained through natural selection. How then, does a lizard evolve a leg into a wing? After all, what is the advantage in half a wing? Even granting that natural processes might favor an ability to fly and thus *preserve* this lizard-becoming-bird—how did the lizard ever *survive* three million years while he was dragging around forelimbs no longer fit for fighting or running, but not yet able to lift him in flight?

These problems have not been lost on the evolutionist. Since the only alternative to evolution is special creation, several new concepts have been beaten out to preserve this "article of faith."

The Second Law of Thermodynamics, known as the entropy law, states that for all closed systems, matter and energy may change in one direction only—that is, from usable to unusable, from concentrated to scattered, from ordered to disordered. In other words, the entropy law states that everything in the universe began with structure and value and is moving irrevocably toward chaos and waste. Automobiles rust out; cities crumble; people age and die. Even a child can see it. It is as much a fact as anything we know.

Enter the evolutionist with a new idea. Call it synergy or syntropy—the built-in tendency toward greater order in nature. Matter just naturally "wants" to perfect itself. Now syntropy, as so far defined, cannot substitute for natural selection. Remember, the fossil record does not show gradual formation of species. Syntropy, therefore, must have another curious property: It does not operate continuously. Massive evolutionary changes are hoarded within the whole community and are only released in bursts at times of stress. Like an electrical capacitor storing up a charge until it is finally loosed in a short span of time, a population of agitated monkeys in part of the jungle rapidly evolves into a tribe of gorillas. This happens so quickly, geologically speaking, that it appears that the gorillas appeared from nowhere. This concept of evolution surging and jerking like a cold engine on a winter morning is called "punctuated equilibrium."

If all this seems a ridiculous construction, I can only note that this is taken very seriously by the scientific community. One professor of paleobiology has written about how fortunate it is that the theory of punctuated equilibrium came along just in time to pull the evolutionists' collective fat from the fire.[20]

More fuel was recently added to the debate in 1988, when geneticists announced the discovery that every human on the planet had descended from a single woman. During the 1960's it was learned that certain parts of living cells—other than the nucleus—contain DNA, which is the hereditary blueprint for cell structure and metabolism. These parts of the cell, called mitochondria, produce the cell's energy and are inherited only from the mother. Since this mitochondrial DNA is not scrambled up each generation by mixing with the father's genes, it can be used to trace family relationships. It turns out that human mitochondrial DNA, while different from that of the apes, is very much alike even across radical and cultural lines. Such differences as exist have been attributed only to genetic mutations.

The scientists made molecular comparisons between many individuals' mitochondrial DNA and, assuming a constant rate of mutation, were able to theorize that we all have a common mother who lived about 200,000 years ago. This finding has been upsetting to the traditional anthropologists. While the 200,000 year figure could be off by 100,000 years or so,

---

20. Steven M. Stanley, *The New Evolutionary Timetable* (New York: Basic Books, Inc., 1981), p. 165.

it cannot be stretched to fit the 10-million-year evolutionary timetable which they had in mind. If that were not bad enough for them, the geneticists have even given our mitochondrial mother a name: "Eve." Still hard at work, the geneticists are confident that in the future they will also discover "Adam."[21]

And yet, the evolutionists stand firm. Nothing will shake their ageless creed, because the alternative, special creation, is unacceptable. Its champions will substitute shamelessly whatever oddly shaped theory they can force into the round hole of the observed facts. It is a matter of faith. Christians also believe by faith, but they have no need for such tortured theories, since Christian faith does not conflict with reason.

Scripture tells us: "I am the Lord, and there is none else: there is no God besides me...I made the earth: and I created man upon it: my hand stretched forth the heavens, and I have commanded all their host." (*Isaias* 45:5, 12).

The impact of this undiscerning faith in biological evolution on the broader beliefs of the New Age will become even clearer in Chapter Four.

Law of Avatars

The beginning of every "New Age" is supposedly initiated by the incarnation of a "god" into a physical body. This *avatar* is a human being who is dominated by the spirit of "The Christ." This century has seen its share of candidates for the office of "The Christ." Some have been unknown, some have been merely laughed at, while one, the German dictator Adolph Hitler, came murderously close to the goal.

On April 25, 1982 a full-page advertisement appeared in major newspapers all around the world. This incredible ad read:

---

21. John Tierney, "The Search for Adam and Eve," *Newsweek*, 11 Jan. 1988, pp. 46-52.

THE WORLD HAS HAD ENOUGH
OF HUNGER, INJUSTICE, WAR.

IN ANSWER TO OUR CALL FOR HELP,
AS WORLD TEACHER FOR ALL
HUMANITY,

THE CHRIST IS NOW HERE.

HOW WILL WE RECOGNIZE HIM?

Look for a modern man concerned with modern problems—political, economic and social. Since July, 1977 the Christ has been emerging as a spokesman for a group or community in a well-known modern country. He is not a religious leader, but an educator in the broadest sense of the word—pointing the way out of our present crisis. We will recognize him by his extraordinary spiritual potency, the universality of his viewpoint, and his love for all humanity. He comes not to judge but to aid and inspire.

WHO IS THE CHRIST?

Throughout history, humanity's evolution has been guided by a group of enlightened men, the Masters of Wisdom. They have remained largely in the remote desert and mountain places of the earth, working mainly through their disciples who live openly in the world. The message of the Christ's reappearance has been given primarily by such a disciple trained for his task for over 20 years. At the center of this "Spiritual Hierarchy" stands the World Teacher, *Lord Maitreya,* known by Christians as the *Christ.* As Christians await the Second Coming, so the Jews await the *Messiah,* the Buddhists the *Fifth Buddha,* the Moslems the *Imam Mahdi,* and the Hindus await *Krishna.* These are all names for one individual. **His presence in the world guarantees there will be no third World War.**

WHAT IS HE SAYING?

"My task will be to show you how to live together peacefully as brothers. This is simpler than you

imagine, My friends, for it requires only the acceptance of sharing.

"How can you be content with the modes within which you now live: when millions starve and die in squalor; when the rich people parade their wealth before the poor; when each man is his neighbor's enemy; when no man trusts his brother?

'Allow me to show you the way forward into a simpler life where no man lacks; where no two days are alike; where the Joy of Brotherhood manifests through all men.

"Take your brother's need as the measure for your action and solve the problems of the world."

WHEN WILL WE SEE HIM?

He has not yet declared his true status, and his location is known to only a very few disciples. One of these has announced that soon the Christ will acknowledge his identity and within the next two months will speak to humanity through a worldwide television and radio broadcast. His message will be heard inwardly, telepathically, by all people in their own language. From that time, with His help, we will build a new world.

WITHOUT SHARING THERE CAN BE NO JUSTICE;
WITHOUT JUSTICE THERE CAN BE NO PEACE;
WITHOUT PEACE THERE CAN BE NO FUTURE.

Thus ran this bold advertisement. The "Christ," of course, did not appear in two months or even in two years. Even if such an appearance did occur, there could be no doubt about his identity. The "Christ" here is not to be confused with Jesus Christ. In this New Age teaching, Jesus was one of many "Christs" who have come upon the earth. But the Bible is very clear regarding the nature of any teaching concerning the identity of Christ: "Who is a liar but he who denieth that Jesus is the Christ. This is Antichrist, who denieth the Father, and the Son." (*1 John* 2:22).

Shortly before Jesus was crucified, the Apostles asked Him

what would be the sign of His coming and the end of the world. He said:

> Take heed that no man seduce you: For many will come in my name saying, I am Christ: and they will seduce many. Then if any man shall say to you: Lo here is Christ, or there, do not believe him. For there shall arise false Christs and false prophets, and shall show great signs and wonders, insomuch as to deceive (if possible) even the elect. (*Matt.* 24:4, 5, 23, 24).

New Age Practices: Yoga, TM & Visualization

New Age meditation includes a variety of related techniques. These are often very similar to the practices of the Hindu and other Eastern religions. Frequently the same practices are, in Western civilization, grouped under the heading of *occultism.* The term is one of pride to the occultists, because it means "hidden." These occult or "hidden" powers of the "ancient wisdom" have supposedly been preserved by the "ascended masters" throughout vast ages of time. It is only in the past hundred years or so that many of these "occultists" have been allowed (by their masters) to write and speak of the ancient wisdom.

Yoga, born in the East, is also widely practiced in the West. Movie stars do it. Athletes and artists do it. Priests, nuns, and even an American archbishop do it. The Hindi word "yoga" comes from the two *Sanskrit* words, "yo" and "ga." "Yoga" means unity. The goal of Yoga is to unite man with the pantheistic god of Hinduism.[22] This union requires a heightened state of consciousness or awareness, during which the yogi realizes his oneness with god or the "higher self." It is oneness with god.

It is being god. As such, from the Hindu perspective it

---

22. Suresh Chander Verma, *Satanic Foundations of Hinduism* (Independence, MO: Jesus Christ Trust, 1983), p. 6

is salvation: No sin. No guilt. No saviour.

There are a number of types of yoga. Most popular in the West is *Raja* Yoga. It is done through meditation and specially designed postures which facilitate the change in consciousness. *Hatha* Yoga is the form of Yoga which deals with these postures and exercises. It is Hatha Yoga which is so often defended as a reliable route to physical fitness. Its advocates often insist that it has no religious aspect that anyone—atheist or Christian—could object to.

Books about Hatha Yoga emphasize strengthening the body, increasing flexibility and endurance, as well as reducing tension. The exercises consist of a series of movements, interrupted by motionless "holds" in the various positions. Even the books that steer away from the spiritual side of Yoga refer to balancing the "life force" so that body, mind and spirit are in harmony.

The position cannot be brushed aside as mere exercises. They were devised long ago for the practice of Hindu meditation and cannot be safely appropriated by Christians. An example is the well-known lotus position. Once the practitioner is seated on the floor, he pulls his legs in close to the hips, with feet resting on the opposite thighs. With the back and head erect and the thumb and index finger pressing together, this position is nearly guaranteed to quiet the mind, slow the breathing, and create a perfect stage for meditation. The erect back and head serve to align what are considered the energy centers, or *chakras,* while the forefinger-thumb contact supposedly prevents the "life force" from dribbling out. Hatha Yoga breathing exercises, such as alternate nostril breathing, supposedly balance this mysterious *prana,* or "life force."

However much Western Yoga practitioners wish to pass off Yoga as a non-religious system, the spiritual nature of Hatha Yoga is undeniable. The ancient *Hatha Yoga Pradipika* records that it was the god Shiva "who expounded the knowledge of Hatha Yoga, which like a staircase leads the aspirant to the high-pinnacled Raja Yoga." The author insists that Raja

Yoga and Hatha Yoga are part of one whole, indispensable to one another. Those who try to separate them, "waste their energy fruitlessly."[23] Sri Aurobindo also taught that every path of Yoga, including Hatha Yoga, has the same goal—unity with the Supreme.[24]

Transcendental Meditation (TM) is the meditative system popularized by the famous guru to the Beatles and others, Maharishi Mahesh Yogi. Called the "Science of Creative Intelligence" (SCI), this method is Hindu meditation parading as science, notwithstanding its adherents' constant claims that "this is not religious."

The student pays his money, receives preparatory instruction and is interviewed by the instructor. Before the actual meditation is taught, the instructor performs a short ceremony designed to thank and honor the chain of meditation teachers ending with the Maharishi's own Guru Dev. They insist, "This is not a religious ceremony." The ritual is performed with various objects—white handkerchief, fruit, and flowers—which the student has brought to the ceremony. It is performed by the teacher and witnessed by the student ("not religious," they still insist).[25] The student is given his secret *mantra,* a Sanskrit word which is repeated during meditation. The meditator begins by concentrating on the mantra only, which is used to drive out all else. Eventually, even the mantra itself disappears from consciousness. Only nothingness or what is called "pure consciousness" remains. The meditation is practiced for 20 minutes twice each day.[26] This state of consciousness bears no relationship to Christian

---

23. *Hatha Yoga Pradipika, Sacred Books of the Hindus* (Allababad, India: Sudhindranatha Vasu, 1915), pp. 1, 27, 58.
24. Sri Aurobindo, *On Yoga I: The Synthesis of Yoga* (Pondicherry, India: Sri Aurobindo Ashram Press, 1957), p. 601.
25. Nat Goldhaber, *An Alphabetical Guide to the Transcendental Meditation Program* (New York: Ballantine Books, 1976), p. 215.
26. *Ibid.,* pp. 51-52.

meditation or to Christian contemplation. This will be more fully explored in the chapter on "The New Age Mystic."

Advanced courses are also available, and in these the religious character of TM is more apparent. The Yoga techniques of posture and breath control are used. The goal is the same.[27] This is not to say that the sellers of TM are lying when they say it is not religious. What they mean is that it involves no teaching of dogma and no overt reference to God. It is a technique.[28] What is not said is that while the dogma is not taught, it will be learned. The changes in one's spiritual perspective and worldview come through the use of the technique. One need not hear the word "Hindu" in order to become one. The United States Third Circuit Court of Appeals is also convinced that SCI/TM is a religion. It upheld a lower court decision bouncing TM classes out of the New Jersey public schools, calling the classes "an establishment of religion."[29]

TM has made incredible claims for itself. A former teacher has sued TM, claiming that the organization promised that in the "Sidhis" course he would learn to "fly" or self-levitate. Moreover, he alleged that he damaged his legs while trying to "fly" (i.e., hopping around in the lotus position) and that he was "permanently psychologically damaged as a consequence of practicing TM."[30] TM's newspaper advertisements offer *increased* intelligence, concentration, memory, creativity, athletic performance and more.[31] If this were not spectacular enough, how about this ad, which the Maharishi's World Government of the Age of Enlightenment ran in *The Wall Street Journal* on August 19, 1983:

---

27. Kenneth Boa, *Cults, World Religions, And You* (Wheaton, IL: Victor Books, 1977), p. 158.
28. Goldhaber, *Alphabetical Guide,* p. 182.
29. Malnak v. Yogi, 592 F.2d 197 (1979).
30. Doe v. Yogi, 652 F. Supp. 203, 209 (D.D.C. 1986).
31. *The Maneater,* February 16, 1988, p. 13.

GOVERNMENTS
INVITED

TO SOLVE THEIR PROBLEMS. THE WORLD GOV-
ERNMENT OF THE AGE OF ENLIGHTENMENT
ANNOUNCES its readiness to solve the problems of any
government regardless of the magnitude and nature of
the problem—political, economic, social, or religious;
and irrespective of its system—capitalism, communism,
socialism, democracy, or dictatorship.

Governments are invited to contract with the World
Government of the Age of Enlightenment to solve their
problems....Complete confidentiality is assured....[32]

———————

TM is just one of many doorways to the altered states of
consciousness essential to New Age thinking. Whether the
altered mental state is brought about by Hindu meditation or
yoga or even through self-help tapes or books teaching self-
hypnosis, the effect is the same. Even the use of drugs may
have the same effect as these techniques. The mind is opened
up to influences which no human can control.

Visualization is the meditator's attempt to manipulate the
world around him. The technique involves a self-induced
trance and the use of the imagination to picture a particular
result in the mind (more on this later). A related technique
is called *guided imagery,* in which the meditator is gently
guided by spoken words into a hypnotic trance. Guided
imagery is more a beginner's technique often used on children
and dispensed with once the student becomes more
"advanced." It is commonly used on New Age "self-help"
tapes and is frequently combined with New Age music to
facilitate the meditation. Both visualization and guided
imagery make this use of imagination. That is not to say that

———————

32. *The Wall Street Journal,* August 19, 1983, p. 19.

there is anything wrong with the common use we make of the imagination in our everyday life. Dave Hunt makes the distinction in his book, *Beyond Seduction:*

> It should be clear that remembering a person, place or event from the past involves mental imagery—and it is just as harmless (and beneficial) to use the imagination to plan something in the future such as a house one hopes to build. Nor is there anything wrong with mentally rehearsing the delivering of a speech or practicing one's golf or tennis swing in the mind. As soon, however, as we think that visualization somehow creates or influences exterior reality (i.e. visualizing the golf ball dropping into the cup will make it happen) or that contact can be made with Jesus or God, we have opened ourselves to possible demonic influences.[33]

Visualization is probably the single most important New Age technique. It is the action side of the movement. Whereas simple meditation purports to *know*, visualization *does*. Without visualization, our material-minded Western society would lose patience with mere meditation. It is the promise of power that lures business people to practice visualization. The same practice that the African "witch doctor," the Siberian *shaman* and the traditional witch rely upon is promoted for the healing of illness, for consulting with spirit "counselors" and to gain material wealth.

There is no Church tradition or Scriptural passage to support the practice of visualization. We are not commanded to go within and create God in our imaginations. Rather, "faith is the substance of things to be hoped for, the evidence of things that appear not." (*Heb.* 11:1). God has condemned divination and sorcery as the tools of the false prophets: "The prophets prophesy falsely in my name: I sent them not, neither have I commanded them, nor have I spoken to them:

---

33. Dave Hunt, *Beyond Seduction: A Return to Biblical Christianity* (Eugene, OR 97402: Harvest House Publishers, 1987), p. 198.

they prophesy unto you a lying vision, and divination, and deceit, and the seduction of their own heart." (*Jer.* 14:14).

We have good cause to reject the technique of visualization. It is deceptive and dangerous. But what if it were not? How can one answer the New Ager whose only response is: "It works!" Leaving one's fate in God's hands is not just obedience; it is wholly practical, for in doing so we choose the greater over the lesser. We trust His visions; not ours. St. Paul reminds us that Christ "is able to do all things more abundantly than we desire or understand, according to the power that worketh in us." (*Eph.* 3:20).

Clearly, even if man *could* create his own reality; even if he were his own god, he must naturally fall short of the glory and happiness which God has in store for him. Dull, weak and colorless by comparison, the universe of the human "god" must be limited by his own puny, wicked imagination. He is eating bologna when he should be eating steak. A motto of the New Agers is, "Whatever the mind can conceive, it can achieve." That is exactly the problem.

New Age Miscellany: Crystals, Rainbows, Channeling, Holistic Health

I will conclude this overview with an assortment of popular New Age ideas and symbols:

Crystals are the real "Pet Rocks." Many New Agers believe in crystal power. Quartz crystals are believed to focus energies in the body, to amplify, balance and harmonize. Other crystals and gemstones of different types and colors are thought to have different effects so that a well-equipped crystal devotée may have a jade for wisdom and tranquillity, a sapphire to elevate the mood and a carnelian to stimulate curiosity. One must learn, though, which crystals complement each other and which should be worn alone. This is, however, no more scientific than astrology, and even if harmless, the use of crystals is just one more rejection of God as the answer for man's spiritual problems.

The *rainbow* is the symbol of God's covenant with men and beasts that He would never again destroy the earth in a flood. (*Gen.* 9:12-17). In the New Age this meaning is discarded, and the rainbow has become a symbol of the Movement. It is known as the *Antahkarana,* or Rainbow Bridge, and represents the bridge of consciousness that each must build between his own mind and soul and the universal mind and soul. It symbolizes realization of oneness with the universe.

One day I was browsing through the gift shop at Unity Village, Missouri near Kansas City. Unity Village is an important New Age center and many Unity members visit there on vacation, perhaps on a pilgrimage of sorts. I overheard a woman next to me admiring a striking crystal shaped like a prism which when placed in a window would spray a rainbow of color across the room. She wanted it, but her husband said, "I thought you said you wanted something that would have real meaning." With that, the woman took him by the arm and pulling him out of earshot gave him (I assumed) the short course of crystals and rainbows. They bought the crystal.

The importance of symbols is more than just to let New Agers find each other. Symbols are used to aid meditation. A person who has learned to meditate with a certain mantra or by using a particular image or place of meditation (real or imagined) will find that the meditation aids will enable him easily and quickly to achieve an altered state of consciousness. Some other New Age symbols are triangles, circles, the sun, crescent moon, and stars—five-pointed, especially upside down—or the star of David, because of the dual triangle structure. There are also the dragon, the unicorn and other mythical creatures; rays of light, the oriental yin/yang symbol, the swastika, enneagram and various perversions of the cross such as the Egyptian anhk and the upside-down cross. Even the number of the Beast of Revelation "666" is found woven into New Age logos.

I want to caution the reader that while the New Agers use these symbols, they do not own all of them. Many are legitimate Christian symbols. Some people just like pretty crystals. A rainbow sticker in the back window does not necessarily mean a New Ager is meditating at the wheel. I once asked an employee of mine what her purpose was in hanging a rainbow from her rear-view mirror. "It's an air freshener," she said. "Keeps the car from stinkin'. Why?"

A few years ago hardly anyone would have known what a *trance channeler* was. Now anyone who saw Shirley MacLaine's TV movie "Out on a Limb" not only knows what channeling is, but witnessed a real trance channeler go into a self-induced trance to enable a spirit being to take over his body. The channeler is what has been called a trance medium in the past. Channelers allow supposed disembodied "ascended masters" to take control of their voice and body and then communicate with onlookers. The messages from these beings are blasphemous toward God and thoroughly New Age in their teachings. If these spirits are genuine, then trance channeling can only be a demonic phenomenon.

It is interesting that *most* New Agers, even the most extreme, like witches, absolutely reject the notion that they follow Satan. And yet, they gladly take marching orders from more "evolved" beings. With the true scheme of things being as it is, what a shock to find out—too late—that Satan, ruler of Hell, is the most "evolved" being of them all.

The *Holistic* (or *Wholistic*) *Health movement* is based on the premise that a person must be seen as a whole being: body, soul (or mind), and spirit. That, in itself, is no revelation. Clearly, the mental and spiritual life affect—and are affected by—the physical body. The problem with the overwhelming bulk of so-called "holistic health" practices lies in the treatments employed to cure the problems on the spiritual side:

- Acupuncture and acupressure (designed to balance the vital energies supposedly coursing

through the body and certain energy centers, or "chakras," as the occultists call them).
- Yoga and Transcendental Meditation.
- Psychic Healing and Therapeutic Touch.
- Use of Crystals and Color Therapy.
- Nutritional therapies based on the supposed spiritual properties of foods.

The obvious reaction to such a list must be that these spiritual "treatments" are not for Catholics. Where is the Catholic list, the one with the prayers, Sacraments and Scripture reading on it? Needless to say, it does not exist. Even if it did, few health professionals would be qualified to apply it. This brand of holistic health is more than a harmless fad. It is spiritually dangerous.

Finally, it would not do to end this chapter without mentioning the mellow music of the New Age. New Age music seems to come in three levels. At the worst, there is the droning hypnotic deep-toned variety. It is distinctive because, in spite of the absence of drums, there is a heavy beat or OM chant running throughout. The mental effect is to induce a hypnotic trance. It works. It leaves one feeling rather dazed and dulled. I have heard Christians who are former New Agers say that it makes them feel seduced and filthy, almost as if they had been molested. On a spiritual level that is a good analogy of the effect upon a Christian.

On the next level, the music is more like a smooth flight above the clouds or a sailboat on a mirrored lake. Usually very pleasant, these synthesized sounds are often blended with natural sounds such as rain or songbirds. The purpose seems to be relaxation, a fertile backdrop for meditation; some go further, purporting to raise one's psychic energy level. The corrupting hypnotic beat of the first type, however, is missing. Even assuming that one does not use the music for occult meditation, and assuming that this *psychic energy* business is false, these recordings still may not be fit for Christian consumption.

The problem is subliminal suggestion. Many New Age artists use subliminal messages which are not consciously heard. This is not conjecture. Some albums not only state that the music contains subliminal messages, but will tell the listener what the messages are. Here are a few real samples:

- "You are a channel for the light."
- "You invoke the blessing of the source of the light."
- "Up, up, higher, higher, fly with me."

Or for specialized purposes:

- "The psychic power you desire is within you and is yours by divine right."
- "You stick to your diet."

The selling point here is that a subliminal message will not be filtered through the rational mind, but instead finds its way inside uninhibited. If subliminal messages work, one can become a New Ager without having made any conscious choice other than to listen to relaxing modern "elevator music." This "middle" type of New Age music may actually be more spiritually damaging than is the first sort, if only because it is disarming.

The third sort of music does not *seem* to be New Age music at all. It sounds normal; it has melody; it goes somewhere during the song and then comes back at the end. It may be that even New Age musicians just get sick of the mindless pabulum they usually play and every once in a while stick in a real tune. Or perhaps the record companies, knowing that New Age music sells, get a little overzealous in attaching the "New Age" label. The safest course may be to stay away from all of it. Certainly, discernment is called for.

2.

Education in the New Age

The theme of the 1985 National Catholic Education Association convention was *Gateway To Global Understanding.* Selected to deliver the keynote address was Robert Muller, at that time Assistant Secretary-General of the United Nations. Promotional literature also listed his name along with the likes of humanist-astronomer Carl Sagan, New Age networker Robert Theobald and several other Globalism/New Age Education advocates. My interest and surprise were sufficient to motivate my registration and attendance at the conference.

The first afternoon Robert Muller set the tone for the meeting. After a number of highly flattering opening remarks he observed that Jesus gave us a universal view because He had come from outer space. Muller reminded the educators that the purpose of the whole conference was for them to implement a global curriculum. He said there was a "need to design a core curriculum for every Catholic school on this planet. I have written such a global core curriculum," he said.

Muller's Curriculum

Muller's "core curriculum" can be found in the July/August and September/October, 1982 editions of *The Beacon,* a publication which describes itself as a "magazine of esoteric philosophy, presenting the principles of the Ageless Wisdom as a contemporary way of life." *The Beacon* is the bi-monthly publication of the openly occult Lucis Trust. Muller organizes his curriculum around the categories of the universe, the human family, our place in time and, lastly, "the miracle of individual human life."[1] The goal, he says, "is to make each child feel like a king or queen in the universe, an expanded being aggrandized by the vastness of our knowledge...."[2] Muller wraps up his global curriculum with a call for good physical, mental, moral and spiritual lives. A good spiritual life he defines as having "spiritual exercises of interiority, meditation, prayer and communion with the universe and eternity or God."[3]

Listening to Muller, it sounds like religion class will never be the same again. One thing I do not recall from my years in the Catholic school was my first "Communion with the Universe." Robert Muller is worth a closer look, especially since his books can be found on the shelves of many Catholic bookstores. Muller's latest book, *New Genesis: Shaping a Global Spirituality,* raises some important questions about this man and why he should be seen as the embodiment of the values that we as Catholics hope to bring into our schools.

His message is that global education must go beyond material, scientific and intellectual achievements and encompass the moral and spiritual spheres. Specifically, the job of global education is to prepare our children for the coming of an interdependent, planetary age, which has supposedly been foretold by all the great prophets.[4]

---

1. Robert Muller, *The Beacon* (New York: Lucis Publishing Company, July/August, 1982), p. 299.
2. Robert Muller, *The Beacon* (New York: Lucis Publishing Company, September/October, 1982), p. 331.
3. *Ibid.,* p. 332.
4. Robert Muller, *New Genesis: Shaping a Global Spirituality* (Garden City, NY: Doubleday Image, 1984), p. 8.

Muller considers himself a good Catholic, but believes that one religion is as good as another. He says: "You are born into a religion and it will give you full satisfaction. Be interested in all religions, in what they have in common, but there is no compelling reason to switch."[5]

Muller had never been deeply religious, so it was not until he became assistant to the late U Thant, former Secretary-General of the U.N., that he was inspired to see life and spirituality bound inextricably together. Buddhist U Thant, whom Muller calls his "spiritual master," caused him to take up the study of Buddhism in order to understand the man better.

"I would never have thought that I would discover spirituality in the United Nations!"[6] he wrote. That "spirituality," as explained in his book, *New Genesis,* is found in the pantheistic religions of Buddhism or Hinduism. He gives us a view of God as a force, a "cosmic" force which is indistinguishable from the universe as a whole. The supposed effect of this force is to exert upward evolutionary pressure upon all mankind to realize that they are divine, that they are God. We have only to realize this great truth. Judge for yourself how well Muller's written word squares with traditional Christianity:

> Our planet, all life on it, and in particular human life, is a manifestation of cosmic or divine forces of the universe. Within us therefore resides a basic cosmic force that impels us to respond to our evolutionary duties. . . .[7]
>
> Humankind is seeking no less than its reunion with the "divine," its transcendence into ever higher forms of life. Hindus call our earth Brahma, or God, for they rightly see no difference between our earth and the divine. This ancient simple truth is slowly dawning again upon humanity.[8]

---

5. *Ibid.,* p. xiii.
6. *Ibid.,* p. 171.
7. *Ibid.,* p. 136.
8. *Ibid.,* p. 49.

> We must elevate ourselves again as light, cosmic beings in deep communion with the universe and eternity. We must re-establish the unity of our planet and of our beings with the universe and divinity. . . .We must see our planet and ourselves as cells of a universe which is becoming increasingly conscious of itself in us. That is our royal road out of the present bewilderment.[9]

Muller's syncretistic groping gives us a "cut & paste" system in which Christianity puts in only a cameo appearance. There is a danger here in proclaiming the equality of all religions. The problem is well expressed by James Hitchcock:

> The religious traditions of the world were [to the devotées of popular religion] like a marvelous tree laden with ripe fruits. They were free to pick and enjoy whatever fruits struck their fancy, to leave those that seemed slightly bitter, and above all never to worry about where the tree came from or how it was nourished and maintained.[10]

It was an incident concerning a man, a woman, a serpent and another fruit-laden tree—along with the dream of being "as gods, knowing good and evil"—that was the beginning of our rebellion. That unhappy episode ended with the man and the woman being driven from Paradise. God cursed the serpent for his role and ordained a future of toil, suffering and sorrow for mankind. This was perhaps the darkest day in human history. Why is it, then, that Robert Muller exults in the shame? He writes:

> We can elicit pride at being humans, at being able, above all species to go so far in the universe. . . .
> Having decided to become like God. . .we have also become masters in deciding between good and bad. . . .[11]

---

9. *Ibid.,* p. 37.
10. James Hitchcock, *What Is Secular Humanism* (Ann Arbor, Michigan: Servant Books, 1982), p. 79.
11. Muller, *New Genesis,* p. 145.

To Muller, it seems, the fall of man turns out to have been a big plus. If we had not chosen to become like God we would not have realized our destiny: to become a showcase in the universe, a planet of God.

Muller's ideas are drawn in part from Teilhard de Chardin. In fact, he has entitled one chapter of his book "My Five Teilhardian Enlightenments," in which he tells the remarkable tale of how he came to hold Teilhard's view of the world. It seems Muller fell into his philosophy as he observed the world through his vantage point at the U.N. At various speaking engagements Muller would find himself blurting out certain ideas of Teilhard such as that "the human species was entering...a period of planetary consciousness" or that he viewed the "earth as a 'living cell.'" At some point he realized that he had experienced his own "Teilhardian Enlightenments" without benefit of Teilhard himself.

Muller's ideas have proved popular with New Age groups such as the Arcane School and World Goodwill. World Goodwill distributes one of Muller's speeches from June, 1989 in which he reminds us where his loyalties lie. Muller advises us to "love the planet and humanity above anything else." But what does Scripture say? "Love not the world," says St. John the Apostle. (*1 John* 2:15). Rather, "Thou shalt love the Lord thy God with thy whole heart, and...soul, and...strength, and...mind: and thy neighbor as thyself." (*Luke* 10:27).

World Goodwill and the Arcane School are affiliated with Lucis Trust, whose publishing branch was originally incorporated as the Lucifer Publishing Company. This openly occult organization is based mainly on the writings of Alice A. Bailey, whose books (she claims) were dictated to her telepathically by the Master Djwhal Khul, who supposedly inhabits the high places in Tibet.

The goals of Lucis Trust include the establishment of a new world order, a new world religion and a new world leader. In their literature this is known as *the plan*.

The plan is directed by so-called "higher intelligences,"

or "the hierarchy." Robert Muller seems to be perfectly comfortable with these masters of wisdom, as he once told the Arcane School how modern science is verifying the proclamations of these "outer space emissaries."[12]

In another speech Muller spoke on the "New Group of World Servers: A Look Into The Future." The New Group of World Servers' role is to prepare us for the New World Christ. Lucis Trust describes the role of the World Servers in the May-June, 1983 issue of *The Beacon:*

> Their work is intended to open up the way to the hierarchy and act as a channel through which can flow the new energies. This, in turn will open up a clear channel for the spirit of peace. . . .This agent of interplanetary love [will] be overshadowing and working through the Christ when he appears. . . .[13]

It should be pointed out that when occultists use the term "Christ" they actually refer to "Lucifer." David Spangler is a board member of the Planetary Initiative For the World We Choose, a grandchild of Robert Muller's Economic and Social Council of the United Nations. Spangler, more than anyone else, has been open about the identity of the "cosmic" forces that Muller so eagerly serves. He writes in his book, *Reflections on the Christ:*

> Christ is the same force as Lucifer. . . .
>
> Lucifer prepares man. . .for the experience of Christhood. . . .
>
> As we move into a new age. . .each of us in some way is brought to that point which I term the *Luciferic Initiation,* the particular doorway through which the individual must pass if he is to come fully into the presence of his light and his wholeness.
>
> Lucifer comes to give us the final. . .Luciferic initia-

---

12. *Ibid.,* p. 121.
13. Dale McKechnie, *The Beacon* (New York: Lucis Publishing Company, May/June, 1983), p. 77.

tion...that many people now and in the days ahead, will be facing, for it is an initiation into the New Age.[14]

And finally, Muller has left a hint concerning the origin of his fruit-laden tree in the conclusion of his book, *New Genesis:*

> And God saw that all nations...were sending their emissaries to a tall glass house...on the island of Manhattan....
>
> And God said: That is good. And it was the first day of the New Age of the earth.
>
> And God saw that the soldiers of peace were separating the combatants of quarreling nations....
>
> And God said: That is good. And it was the second day....[15]

This recital continues quite predictably. Throughout all seven days (not six), we humans brilliantly eradicate hunger and ignorance, waste and bigotry. On the seventh day God and man together are restored as the *Alpha* and *Omega* and what we had always thought was a throne turns out to be a love seat. Never mind, God obligingly scoots over and announces that this, too, is good. As mankind basks in its self-generated glory, Muller puts these final words into God's mouth:

> I will now make My peace with you and let you establish a perfect Earth. Farewell, My grownup children. At long last you are on the right path, you have brought heaven down to earth and found your proper place in the universe. I will now leave you for a long journey, for I have to turn my sight to other troubled and unfinished celestial bodies. I now pronounce you Planet of God. Be happy.[16]

---

14. David Spangler, *Reflections on the Christ* (Findhorn, Scotland: 1978), pp. 40-44.

15. Muller, *New Genesis,* p. 190.

16. *Ibid.,* p. 191

Now I do not know how Robert Muller's Bible ends, but mine does not have God riding off into the sunset. As I read the above passage it struck me first as being just some more typically saccharine New Age rubbish. And then... no; far more fitting are these words in the mouth of Satan, spoken at that moment of final ruin. He fancies himself corrupting other worlds when he has finished with ours. My Bible disagrees on another point also: Satan's end is clearly pictured in the prophetic Book of the Apocalypse: "And there came down fire from God out of heaven, and devoured them; and the devil, who seduced them, was cast into the pool of fire and brimstone, where both the beast and the false prophet shall be tormented day and night for ever and ever."

We can understand why pagans would be interested in spreading this cosmic, global gospel. But the question is, what are Christians doing fooling around with such nonsense? And how long will we Christians tolerate feeding this lie to our children?

National Catholic Education Association

It would not be so bad if the 1985 convention stood alone as an aberration. But the Movement in Catholic education did not begin in 1985, nor is it over now. Even a sympathetic New Age source admits that the effect to undermine the nation-state system and implement global thinking goes back at least fifteen years:

> The NCEA launched a "Peace Education" program in 1972 which seeks to develop a global consciousness among its member educators, thus laying the basis for developing a planetary framework for integrated curricula development.[17]

---

17. Gerald and Patricia Mische, *Toward a Human World Order* (New York/Ramsey, NY: Paulist Press, 1977), p. 308.

If the only questionable speaker at the 1985 NCEA convention had been Robert Muller, it would be bad enough. Unfortunately, Muller was only a fragment of the picture, albeit an important one.

Another speaker was John I. Goodlad, who presented "Restructuring the Educational Process." Goodlad is a realist who assumes from the outset that Catholic parents will not like "global education." In the foreword to James Becker's book, *Schooling for a Global Age,* Goodlad cautions:

> Parents and the general public must be reached also. Otherwise, children and youth may find themselves *in conflict with values assumed in the home.* And then the educational institution frequently comes under scrutiny and must pull back.[18]

Carl Sagan, of COSMOS fame, insulted every Catholic in the house during his talk about "nuclear winter." Given the fact that true Christians have always been willing to die for their faith, the surprise was that Sagan was applauded when he suggested that no religion (or political belief) was worth dying for.

Another very popular speaker was Dolores Leckey, Executive Director of the U.S. Bishops' Committee on the Laity. The preliminary convention program described her as:

> A great spokesperson for every Catholic woman... someone whose spirituality and sense of meaning has been strongly shaped by her Catholic roots, but who has dared to explore other sources of wisdom as well...a typical female Catholic of the '50s who broke the mold.

In her speech to the general session, she approvingly cited writer and lecturer Rosemary Haughton, saying: "She is pointing to the new physics...and to the wisdom of the East

---

18. James Becker, *Schooling for a Global Age,* foreword by John I. Goodlad (New York: McGraw Hill, 1979), p. xvii (emphasis added).

as a means of recovering that which has been lost...a new alternative social order."

I always sit up straight and listen when Christian speakers defer to "the wisdom of the East." She began to explain how Our Lord was able to work His healing miracles: "He [Jesus] perceived in others the operation of the same divine energy that was his own motive power. He knew people...as possessing the same power he had."

Leckey further explained that when Jesus told people that their faith had healed them:

> He was acknowledging the power of the transaction, a flowing of knowledge and power between them. His compassion was an essential agent, it is true, yet one that was powerless, in a sense, without the response that somehow completed the circuit and transformed the situation. Jesus found himself able to liberate the divine energy in people over and over again. When he did this it produced a psycho-physical transformation that came neither from him nor from the other person. It was not isolated in that way, but was the fruit of their encounter....Though it seems at times that he tried to contain the phenomenon...it simply couldn't be done.

According to Leckey, it was as if Jesus were a mere man who happened to find himself "able to liberate the divine energy," who could not "contain the phenomenon," and who was powerless without the "response that...completed the circuit."

But faith is not power. It is not even half of the power. If that were so, then how did Our Lord raise the dead? Certainly a dead body has no faith. At the pool of Siloe (Siloam) the man born blind made no expression of faith, but instead seemed to serve purely as a demonstration of the power of God. (*John* 9:1-7).

It is the belief of those who practice the so-called "mind powers" that faith is power in itself. In effect, one must have faith in his faith. But faith must have an object, and more, that faith must be in the correct object. Someone has said that given the problem of crossing a deep gorge, one would do better crossing a strong bridge, though frightened and unsure of its strength, than to cross a fatally weakened bridge with confidence. If the object of faith is correct, the faith will be rewarded.

At another session, New Age author Robert Theobald spoke about "The New Technologies and Global Education." His talk was concerned with the ways he felt we must all change in the future, how we must teach "holistically" and teach "values." Before leaving the convention I picked up a little volume called *At the Crossroads,* at a booth attended by Sister Judith Bisignano (more on this interesting lady shortly). Although the book was authored by a committee, the Sister told me that Theobald was the chief writer. *At the Crossroads* turns out to be a New Age manifesto. Just a few of the concepts embraced:

- subordination of the needs of nations to needs of the planet
- interdependence and connectedness of all things
- government by an elite few
- visualization
- development of new governmental boundaries

Unfortunately, there was no suggestion that what we are to be "subordinated" to and "interconnected" with has any relation to Jesus Christ, who is God—except perhaps to deny His authority over man. The document is signed by many New Age notables, and the list of recommended resources is loaded with New Age references:

- Marilyn Ferguson's *Leading Edge Bulletin*
- Mark Satin's *New Options* newsletter
- Marilyn Ferguson's *The Aquarian Conspiracy*
- John Naisbitt's *Megatrends*
- Donald Key's *Earth at Omega*
- Peter Russell's *The Global Brain*
- Fritjof Capra's *The Turning Point*

Kino Learning Center

One last example will serve to complete this short review of the 1985 NCEA convention. Sister Judith Bisignano, O.P., Ed.D., offered the blatantly New Age speech, "A Working Model of New Age Learning." Sister Bisignano is the founder of the Kino Learning Center of Tucson, Arizona. The Kino Learning Center, Inc. is a "Catholic" elementary and secondary school founded in 1975.

The Sister spoke mostly about the New Age philosophy that she and her colleagues bring to the school and how Kino puts that philosophy into action. She appealed to the teachers present to take the lead in bringing in the New Age. She began with her opinion that:

> Children are an oppressed minority, and certainly Catholic schools have the ability, have the freedom...to be leaders of...the new age model.
>
> Things have to change drastically...If this happens....Catholic schools will become a major leader in the regeneration of society.

A few traditional skills (like reading and writing) are required for graduation, but for the most part students at Kino are free to learn only what they wish to learn—or to learn absolutely nothing: "Children should have the freedom to do nothing," the Sister told us. This is called a "child-centered" classroom situation. Someone asked whether the children must learn certain truths such as the Resurrection. Sister Bisignano said, "If the topic...doesn't interest him then he's not going to learn about the Resurrection."

She says that if the child does not *choose* to study it in her school, then neither would he learn about it in a conventional classroom. A question concerning the teaching of the Ten Commandments was asked, and Sister answered:

"If the child is not interested in the Ten Commandments today, then he doesn't have to learn them. The power is in the child to direct his life."

"But is it possible," asked one teacher, "that the child

might never learn the Ten Commandments?"

The answer was affirmative: "You could get through Kino without choosing to study the Ten Commandments."

The Sister was not apologetic. Instead, she seemed to lament the fact that they were required to teach certain things (such as reading and the other basics). She confessed that she herself hated to read, considered it pure drudgery, and felt that the day would soon come when the children need not learn to read at all. In the meantime, though, Kino does provide the opportunity to read.

She said what she really wanted was to teach the values that would hold the children in good stead in the New Age. These values were taught through a series of workbooks which she proudly displayed on the dais. Sister Bisignano said she longed for the day when those workbooks would be all that needed to be taught. One workbook, *Living With Death,* exposes the student to the concepts of suicide and euthanasia without giving him real guidance as to the right and wrong of it. One project has the student writing a "living will" in which the student proclaims that death is preferable to the "indignities" of illness and demands "mercifully administrated" medication "to alleviate suffering even if it may hasten the moment of death."

Other exercises involve the student in visiting mortuaries, writing out the funeral invoice for his own burial, designing tombstones, writing obituaries, donating organs and doing death crossword puzzles (*hint:* 12 DOWN is reincarnation).[19]

One page dealt with life after death. It explained that many people believe that each person (and sometimes animals, plants, rocks and rivers) have a spirit within:

> Some people believe that the soul goes to a spirit land, sometimes called Paradise or Heaven, where perfect happiness exists. Some people believe that a spirit leaves

---

19. Judith Bisignano, O.P., Ed.D., *Living With Death* (Kansas City, MO: Sheed & Ward, 1985), pp. 36-41, 46, 48, 50-55.

a dying person and enters the body of a baby that is being born. Other people believe that a human spirit finds a home in some animal—a bird, a cow, or a dog. These beliefs of a spirit living again in another person or animal are called reincarnation.

If you believe in life after death, use words and pictures to describe what you think this might be like.[20]

The bottom half of the page was left open for drawing whatever the student wished. The exercise did not suggest which view was the correct one.

Another Kino workbook, *Creating Your Future,* has a foreword by Robert Theobald. The opening and closing exercises are tests of the students' awareness and acceptance of New Age concepts taught in the workbook. In between are lessons designed to induce fidelity to a New Age platform (global consciousness, a new world order, the doctrine of unlimited human potential).[21]

None of the above was done in a vacuum. Present at the conference were several American archbishops, including Milwaukee Archbishop Rembert Weakland. While there was no lack of criticism of the agenda, unfortunately none of it came from the archbishops. The organizers of the event dismissed all dissent as coming from a narrow-minded minority. Sister Mary Ann Eckhoff, superintendent of schools for the archdiocese of St. Louis, explained the rationale: "We may not agree with everything we hear [at the conference], but we don't grow up in a cocoon. . . . Catholic educators are sophisticated enough to sift out truth."

As an editorial[22] in one Catholic periodical commented, "Teachers who attend the NCEA meeting will just have to

---

20. *Ibid.,* p. 33.
21. Judith Bisignano *et al., Creating Your Future: Activities to Encourage Thinking Ahead* (Tucson, AZ: Kino Learning Center, 1985), pp. iii, 1, 35, 61.
22. *The Wanderer,* April 18, 1985 (St. Paul, MN: Wanderer Printing Co.), p. 4.

sort out for themselves what is poisonous and antithetical to Catholicism and what is not."

For several years following the 1985 convention, the New Age themes cut a narrower swath at NCEA conventions. The globalist/New Age presentations became inconspicuous, and were limited to the workshops. Whenever there are *useful* workshops to attend, few teachers willingly show up in these New Age sideshows. To reach the teachers, the New Agers need the captive audience of the convention's general sessions to communicate their message effectively. Being stuck in the workshops is a high hurdle for the New Agers to overcome when the general sessions are encouraging authentic Catholic teaching and basic fundamentals.

Unfortunately, the New Age found its opening again with the address of Jean Houstin, Ph.D. to the 1989 NCEA convention. Dr. Houston, founder of The Foundation for Mind Research, spoke in the general session.

Dr. Houston is past-president of the mystical/occult-oriented Association of Humanistic Psychology and a member of the International Advisory Board of the Oasis Center of Chicago. The Oasis Center's holistic schedule includes programs on Yoga, Shamanism, Healing Touch, I Ching, and the "Goddesses in Everywoman."[23] In 1988, the center offered Houston's own seminar: "Pangaia: Whole System Transition and the Earth's New Story: A Mythic Event."[24]

Jean Houston has co-authored the book *Mind Games,* a series of group explorations into altered states of consciousness. Scattered throughout the book are graphic images accompanied by the words WAKE UP! Houston explains that the "mind games" in the book (intended for group sessions) will also induce a trance in some readers. Readers wishing to terminate the trance need only look at the image, clap hands and say "WAKE UP!" In this book, Jean Houston

---

23. *Oasis Center,* January-March, 1989.
24. *Oasis Center,* July-September, 1988.

teaches the sorcerer's techniques of visualization and even materialization of an entity she calls "the Group Spirit." This entity, which is conjured up during a deep group "shared trance," is described as perceptible to all the senses, including touch. The "players" establish a rapport with the spirit entity, which takes and answers questions.[25]

She has predicted that "in our lifetime we will see the rise of essentially a new world religion. . . . I believe a new spiritual system will emerge. . . ."[26] Jean Houston has recounted how, as a young girl, she was influenced in her talks with an elderly man she called "Mr. Teller." Only later did she learn that the man she had befriended as a schoolgirl in New York City's Central Park was Pierre Teilhard de Chardin.[27]

Undoubtedly there are individuals within the NCEA still dedicated to spreading the New Age infection to the Catholic schools. As long as New Age luminaries such as Muller and Houston are welcomed by NCEA, the contest will not be won. One thing is certain; those fouled with the New Age creed will not go quietly. The prize is too big.

The underlying motive behind this push for the Globalist-New Age agenda stems from the unique position occupied by the Catholic Church. In a real sense—and Robert Muller said as much in his keynote address to our Catholic school teachers—the Church is the big prize. The Catholic Church, with its worldwide school system, has been targeted as the most potent vehicle possible in bringing in the New Age. The prize is not unwinnable by the New Agers, because while the Catholic Church will remain in some form until the Second Coming, that does not insure that the decay will not be

---

25. Robert Masters and Jean Houston, *Mind Games* (New York: Viking Press, 1972), pp. 198-206.
26. Texe Marrs, *Dark Secrets of the New Age* (Westchester, Illinois: Crossway Books, 1987), p. 40, quoting Jean Houston, interviewed in "Jean Houston: The New World Religion," *The Tarrytown Letter,* June/July 1983, p. 5.
27. Muller, *New Genesis,* pp. 167-168.

far advanced. And to whatever extent the Church is itself preserved, individual dioceses, parishes and schools do not have a divine guarantee of preservation. It is not to the Church that Our Lord will say, "Depart from Me," but to individuals. Eternal life, while won by the death and Resurrection of Christ, is chosen by individuals, one at a time. There has never been an age for serene, witless indifference to what the Church really teaches, and ours is no exception. We as individuals still have to know and practice our faith in order to be saved. There is no assurance from Scripture or anywhere else that God will protect a stubborn and corrupted people from a false movement which threatens to overtake and swallow them.

The Local Catholic School

There has been much talk about the shortage of vocations and the increasing importance of an active laity. All parents should be involved with what their children are learning in school.

It does not take long to look over a religion textbook. Look for minimizing of the deity of Christ and distortions of the fact of sin; look for the equating of Christianity with all other religions—or worse, the actual criticism of Christianity in comparison to the so-called "higher" religions of Hinduism and Buddhism. While you are looking, notice what is not there: the authority of the Church and the Scriptures, the reality of Heaven, Hell and Purgatory, the fact of the biblical miracles—and look for a general lack of guidance for the child's moral growth.

A Catholic textbook for older students need not ignore other religions, but there is an obligation to point to the truth. A "neutral" lesson is not neutral at all, because it teaches that all religions are equal. That is not Catholicism. That is the New Age religion.

Talk to your children to find out what they are doing in religion class. William C. Brown Company, the same publisher that brought us the widely (and properly) criticized elementary sex education series, *New Creation,* has produced *Guided Meditations for Children,* written by Jane Reehorst, B.V.M. Subtitled, "How to Teach Children to Pray Using Scripture," the meditations are recommended for use with the "Light of Faith" series, also from Wm. C. Brown. These meditations use "guided imagery," a form of visualization. At first, the technique looks like simple story-telling, but it is much more.

The teacher allows the children to choose body positions which will establish their commitment to prayer and will be conducive to comfort and relaxation. The teacher is encouraged to begin with the meditation, "Meeting Jesus." This establishes that place in the child's imagination where he can go to meet Jesus whenever he wishes. This same device is used in the Silva Mind Control Method (see Chapter Seven) to facilitate meditation and visualization. Silva calls this special place the "laboratory." For the rest of the school year the "prayer" time is begun with the words, "Let us go to our place to meet Jesus." The class is encouraged to go to that place whenever they want.[28]

A meditation begins: "Close your eyes (pause). Take a deep breath (pause) and relax (pause). You are walking with Jesus and His disciples. . . ." The teacher "guides" the children through the experience. They play with Jesus. He talks. The child talks and plays. All of this is like a story until abruptly the teacher says, "I'll leave you alone with Jesus to begin your game of celebration." And just like that the teacher saws off the limb and the child is left alone with his visions. You can see that "guided imagery" is guided only to a point. After a time the teacher says a prayer and tells the children, "It is time to leave. . . .Say good-bye to Jesus. . . .and begin to walk away. . . .Open your eyes and come back to the room."[29]

---

28. Jane Reehorst, B.V.M., *Guided Meditation: How to Teach Children to Pray Using Scripture* (Dubuque, Iowa: Wm. C. Brown, 1986), p. vi.
29. *Ibid.,* p. 11.

The children are back from their hypnotic trance, but there is one more New Age chore to perform before finishing. The children finish each meditation by writing down their responses to these visualizations of Jesus.[30] If it were not enough that the children are initiated into guided (and unguided) meditation, the text the teacher uses is three-fourths fantasy, with little if any indication that Jesus is more than a nice man to play with. Subtle distortions come in. At the wedding feast at Cana, the child is present and sees Mary come up and speak to Jesus. Later a servant brings wine, apologizing for the delay. "For awhile we thought we ran out of wine," he says, "but now we have plenty."[31] That scene has meaning for you and me, but then we know the story. Too bad the child does not get the point.

During another meditation, the child finds himself at the feeding of the multitudes. Jesus says, "Pass this out to the people," so the child and the Apostles begin to pass out the loaves and fishes. But there is a discrepancy: "Soon your bread is gone." Jesus shares His food with the child. There are twelve baskets of food left over. The lesson: "When one shares God's gifts there is always enough to go around."[32] Once again, you have to get the feeling that someone is hiding the ball here. Is it necessary to paper over the obvious miracle that occurred in order to teach children to share?

If your child is exposed to New Age ideas and meditations in school, you are the one that must do something. Talk to the pastor. Talk to the school board. Talk to the bishop. You may be surprised by the appreciation of those unaware of the problem. On the other hand, be prepared to be ignored, or worse, insulted. Some parents have been not-so-politely told to shut up or get their children out of the school. But these are *our* children, and there is no one else to stand up. Very

---

30. *Ibid.,* p. vi.
31. *Ibid.,* p. 10.
32. *Ibid.,* pp. 25-27.

likely it is the lay person, the parent and courageous Catholic school teachers who must take up the challenge and withstand the attack of those who would use and then destroy the Church. Power is not measured by the letters after one's name, but by obedience to God. The battle is not hopeless. As the Apostle Paul reminds us:

> Finally, brethren, be strengthened in the Lord, and in the might of his power. Put you on the armour of God, that you may be able to stand against the deceits of the devil. For our wrestling is not against flesh and blood; but against principalities and powers, against the rulers of the world of this darkness, against the spirits of wickedness in the high places. (*Eph.* 6:10-12).

3.

Priest or Guru?

*When thou art come into the land which the Lord thy God shall
give thee, beware lest thou have a mind to imitate the abominations
of those nations. Neither let there be found among you any
one...that consulteth soothsayers, or observeth dreams and omens,
neither let there be any wizard, nor charmer, nor any one that consulteth pythonic spirits, or fortune tellers, or that seeketh the truth
from the dead. For the Lord abhorreth all these things, and for these
abominations he will destroy them at thy coming.* (Deut. 18:9-12).

It is a common question: Why do people (especially religious and clergy), when they no longer believe in the faith
they espouse, insist upon remaining in and influencing the
Church? In the Catholic Church there are many truths which
one must accept. To deny these is to relinquish the right to
the name "Catholic" or even "Christian." The famous Anglican writer C.S. Lewis once gave a speech to an assembly of
Anglican ministers and youth leaders. He asked them to
respect the boundary lines:

> I think it is your duty to fix the lines clearly in your
> own minds: and if you wish to go beyond them you must
> change your profession.
> This is your duty not specially as Christians or as
> priests but as honest men. There is a danger here of the
> clergy developing a special professional conscience

which obscures the very plain moral issue. Men who have passed beyond these boundary lines in either direction are apt to protest that they have come by their unorthodox opinions honestly. In defence of those opinions they are prepared to suffer obloquy and to forfeit professional advancement. Thus they come to feel like martyrs. But this simply misses the point which so gravely scandalizes the layman. We never doubted that the unorthodox opinions were honestly held: what we complain of is your continuing your ministry after you have come to hold them. We always knew that a man who makes his living as a paid agent of the Conservative Party may honestly change his views and honestly become a Communist. What we deny is that he can honestly continue to be a Conservative agent and to receive money from one party while he supports the policy of another.[1]

Whether a Catholic can apostatize "honestly" and without moral blame is one question. On the other hand, we have every right to demand that a Catholic, especially one with a teaching office, who chooses to become (for example) more Hindu than Ghandi, have the courage and honesty to dissociate from the Church.

Is it possible that the most "Christian" view is one that admits that all religions are paths to God? On the surface that seems the most loving, open and kind interpretation. But it can do no good to insist that all paths lead to God if, in fact, they do not. It is Our Lord Himself who declares:

Enter ye in at the narrow gate: for wide is the gate, and broad is the way that leadeth to destruction, and many there are who go in thereat. How narrow the gate, and strait is the way that leadeth to life: and few there are that find it! (*Matt.* 7:13-14).

So-called open-minded people rail against the "one way"

---

1. C.S. Lewis, *God in the Dock* (Grand Rapids, MI: William B. Eerdmans Publishing, 1970), p. 90.

viewpoint that true Christianity teaches, and in doing so they reject the sacrifice of Jesus Christ.

Before His death all mankind was lost to sin, separated from God by an impassable gulf. It is as if Christ came to build a bridge over which everyone could cross. Even though He paid the highest possible price to build that one bridge, there are those who insist that He build innumerable others. They would accuse God of cruelty if He were to punish people who refuse the provision made by Jesus Christ. *Cruel* is a better description for these open-minded ones who, in effect, would crucify Jesus again and again.

We have been commanded: "Teach ye all nations; baptizing them in the name of the Father, and of the Son, and of the Holy Ghost." (*Matt.* 28:19). The tragedy is that so many priests and religious no longer see this as their commission. They work to change the world, when they ought first to be working to save souls. This pattern, typical of popular ideas today, is not the biblical one. Instead, the truth is made a lie as the proper sequence is inverted; our order of priorities has become perfectly and completely reversed. The world says: Take care of material needs first. Only then can spiritual needs be met. Our Lord says: "Seek ye therefore first the kingdom of God, and his justice, and all these things shall be added unto you." (*Matt.* 6:33).

In an article from the Jesuit magazine *America*, Denis Murphy reported on a new way to look at evangelism. From the Cardinal of Karachi, Pakistan: "Conversions are not the most important...Rather our task is to give an extraordinarily clear witness to our Christian values, especially in social matters of justice and honesty."[2] A bishop in Bangladesh says, "Islam and Hinduism are salvific, for how could the good God abandon them." Even in the sharing of his faith he says he does it because he values the faith, not because the pagans need it.[3]

Consider the faulty logic of one Indian Jesuit theologian

2. Denis Murphy, *America* (August 25, 1979).
3. *Ibid.*

who argues: "The fact that members of the higher religions, such as Hindus and Buddhists, do not convert may be a sign that they are not meant to convert."[4] One might as well conclude that the fact that a man is starving may be a "sign" that he was not "meant" to eat.

These are the Modernists of our day, and like those condemned eighty years ago by Pius X in *Pascendi,* they "do not deny, but actually maintain, some confusedly, others frankly, that all religions are true."[5] The arguments of the Modernists are merely unconvincing end-runs around such compelling biblical injunctions as the Great Commission, or this simple reasoning by St. Paul: "For whosoever shall call upon the name of the Lord, shall be saved. How then shall they call on him, in whom they have not believed? Or how shall they believe him, of whom they have not heard? And how shall they hear, without a preacher? And how shall they preach unless they be sent?" (*Rom.* 10:13-15).

It is the conventional wisdom of the mission field that the missionary must learn of the ways, language and culture of the people he would convert. The situation in the East has gone a step further, and we find that it is the pagan that has instead converted the missionary. Jesuit priests have started imitating the Hindu holy men, taking the title "swami" and wearing saffron robes and sporting begging bowls. The so-called "Indian rite" uses the mantra "OM," the name of the Hindu god Krishna.[6] Fr. Bede Griffiths is one of these Christian gurus.

Fr. Bede Griffiths

The initial religious formation of Dom Bede Griffiths, O.S.B. was minimally Anglican. Of immense influence upon

---

4. *Ibid.,* p. 75.
5. Pius X, *Pascendi,* p. 16.
6. Malachi Martin, *The Jesuits* (New York: Linden Press, 1987), p. 411.

him was his early reading of the Hindu *Bhagavad Gita* and other books of Eastern spiritual wisdom introduced to him by a friend of his mother. This friend, who was to have such a strong effect on him, was a Theosophist and suffragette who shocked children by smoking cigarettes.[7]

Griffiths, once a student of C.S. Lewis at Oxford, converted from unbelief to Catholicism at about the same time Lewis was undergoing his own conversion to Anglican Christianity. He entered a Benedictine monastery within a few weeks of his conversion and was later ordained a priest.

Bede Griffiths had assumed that he would preach the Gospel, but learned he could not teach that which he was still searching for. He went to India to help found a monastery, and never left. His community, called *Shantivanam* ("Forest of Peace"), is affiliated with the Benedictine community of Camaldoli in Italy, but follows the customs of a Hindu ashram, with Griffiths as guru.[8] He says: "Certainly from a Christian point of view the importance of Indian philosophy can hardly be overestimated. It marks the supreme achievement of the human mind in the natural order in its quest of a true conception of God."[9]

Griffiths calls the Hindu temple a "sacrament" and is caught up in admiration for these people who have so penetrated the "ultimate mystery." In the temple of Shiva the destroyer, the innermost holy place contains the lingam or phallus where the worshipper communes with the ultimate reality.[10]

He claims that it is easy to meet the Hindu on the level of liturgy, language, music and art, but very difficult to meet him on a theological level. Nevertheless, Fr. Griffiths believes that the task is possible. Unfortunately, this is only

---

7. Bede Griffiths, *The Golden String* (New York: P.J. Kenedy and Sons, 1954), p. 58.
8. Harrison Hoblitzelle, *New Age Journal*, "A Visit with Father Bede Griffiths: INDIA'S CHRISTIAN GURU," August, 1983, p. 40.
9. Bede Griffiths, *The Golden String*, p. 152.
10. Bede Griffiths, *Christ in India* (New York: Charles Scribner's Sons, 1966), p. 99

accomplished by subordinating Christianity to Hinduism. He accuses Christians of having an imperfect understanding of Christ (which may be true), but he then proceeds to send us to Hindus and Muslims to clear up our misunderstandings.[11] In the end he sees no rationale for preaching the Gospel, for at bottom we are all believers. Fr. Griffiths says:

> No one can say in the proper sense that the Hindu, the Buddhist or the Muslim is an "unbeliever." I would say rather that we have to recognize him as our brother in Christ...
>
> Our task in India is not so much to bring Christ to India (as though he could be absent), as to discover Christ already present and active in the Hindu soul.[12]

Fr. Edward Hays

We should not think, however, of this phenomenon of priests becoming gurus as only happening halfway around the world. We have our own priest-gurus here in the United States. One is Fr. Edward Hays, who is widely recognized as an expert on prayer.

Formerly a parish priest, he was sent on a year-long pilgrimage by his archbishop. Fr. Hays had requested a few months off for prayer in a Christian monastery, but his bishop, now Archbishop Ignatius Strecker of Kansas City, Kansas, had other ideas. He suggested that Fr. Hays take a year off to travel in search of new ideas. Fr. Hays was advised to go also to the non-Christian religions in his quest for freshness in spirituality. The Archbishop hoped that Fr. Hays would found a "house of prayer" upon his return. He traveled to the Middle East and the Orient as a prayer pilgrim seeking wisdom.

For more than sixteen years, Fr. Hays has run his Catholic-Hindu "house of prayer," which is financially supported by

11. *Ibid.*, pp. 183, 189.
12. *Ibid.*, pp. 196, 217.

the Catholics of Archbishop Strecker's archdiocese. The name of his retreat house is "Shantivanam," the same as the name of Bede Griffiths' ashram in India.[13]

The chapel at Shantivanam is a tiered, octagonal room with a decidedly Eastern flavor. We interrupt a young man's Yoga meditation as we enter the chapel. The altar (an old wooden horse manger) stands on bare earth facing neat rows of oriental prayer rugs. Lit by candles and sunlight, and scented with incense, the room is a museum of religious evolution.

Fr. Hays' system is pure syncretism. He blends Christianity with the other religions and puts Jesus in the same class as "Buddha and the other holy saviors. . ."[14] In a layout reminiscent of the Stations of the Cross, one side of the chapel holds a shrine to Shiva, Hindu god of destruction. Next on this wall is a Buddha, followed by a copy of the Scriptures, the Tabernacle of the Blessed Sacrament, a picture of Our Lady of Guadalupe, and finally, a crucifix. The purpose is to give due honor to each progressive revelation. The large windows wrap around one end of the chapel to give a beautiful panorama of the forest and fields.

With the wide assortment of gods available here, a worshipper could get confused. Nevertheless, the goddess of Shantivanam receives her due, because the goddess of Shantivanam is Creation. Nature is the theme that claims the field of vision here: the expanse of windows and the altar dug into the dirt. This is creation-centered spirituality.

Hays is typically Eastern in his teachings. He recommends the use of a mantra, proper breathing and special sacred places for meditation.[15] Speaking of our "new spirit of sexuality," he says: "We must trust our inner voices even when they assert that there is goodness and beauty in what past ages

---

13. *The Catholic Key,* "KEY Welcomes Fr. Ed Hays As A New Contributing Columnist" (April 21, 1985).
14. Edward Hays, *Secular Sanctity* (Easton, KS: Forest of Peace Books, 1984), p. 16.
15. *Ibid.,* p. 101.

have called evil and dirty."[16]

See how this inverts the words of Isaias (5:20):

> Woe to you that call evil good, and good evil:
> that put darkness for light, and light for darkness:
> that put bitter for sweet, and sweet for bitter.

In his newspaper columns he has done the same thing: Turn the Scriptures (the Christian Bible) upside down. Most often it is the Oriental scriptures which he quotes, and then with earnest reverence. In one story, Fr. Hays portrays a king who refuses Heaven unless God lets both his dog and his unbelieving family into Heaven with him. The stubborn king wins out, and God praises the king's faithfulness as He allows them all in.[17] Once again the truth is the exact opposite, for Our Lord said:

> He that loveth father or mother more than me, is not
> worthy of me; and he that loveth son or daughter more
> than me, is not worthy of me. And every one that hath
> left house, or brethren, or sisters, or father, or mother,
> or wife, or children, or lands for my name's sake, shall
> receive a hundredfold, and shall possess life everlasting.
> (*Matt.* 10:37, 19:29).

While the flavor of the East dominates Shantivanam, the Western pagan traditions are not ignored. A former staff member has related that, "On occasion, ancient festivals of the Celts or Saxons are remembered and members dance round a may pole or a fire pit in the fields or forest."[18] Even a druid or a witch could feel at home in a place like this! But pagan idols and Celtic festivals aside, business at this archdiocesan "house of prayer" is quite good. Shantivanam can barely accommodate visitors from outside the Archdiocese.

---

16. *Ibid.*, p. 80.
17. Edward Hays, *The Catholic Key* (April 21, 1985).
18. Ron Miller and Jim Kinney, *Fireball and the Lotus* (Santa Fe, New Mexico: Bear & Co., 1987), p. 195 (article by Michael Hugo).

Thomas Merton

This chapter would not be complete without some comment about the man who has been so influential in transforming a key segment of the Catholic Church—the contemplative orders. The man is Thomas Merton. He has been described as "an Englishman who became a Communist, then a Catholic, later a Trappist monk, and finally a Buddhist, at which point, his life having been fulfilled, he died."[19] There was little about Merton's life—whether before or after his conversion—that could be called orthodox. He viewed the Catholic life as inducing "all forms of neurosis and anxiety."

"The way the Christian life is lived," he said, "is so schizophrenic that it is a wonder one can be at the same time a Christian and sane."[20]

Merton's pre-occupation was with mystical experience. His over-reaching assumption was that all such experiences were valid and self-authenticating, regardless of their source. To him, the inner journeys of all religions were equally true. Merton wanted to see a synthesis among the religious traditions of the world. Shortly before his death, he wrote an admiring introduction to a new translation of the *Bhagavad Gita*, the most important of the Hindu scriptures.

His last journey was to the Orient, in 1968, at the time of the first World Spiritual Summit conference sponsored by the Temple of Understanding. As he departed the U.S., Merton said he left with "a great sense of destiny, of being at last on my way after years of waiting and wondering and fooling around."[21] (Remember, Merton had spent the previous 27 years as a Trappist monk at Gethsemani, in Kentucky— apparently, as he wrote, "fooling around.")

---

19. Edward Rice, *The Man in the Sycamore Tree: The Good Times and Hard Life of Thomas Merton* (Garden City, NY: Doubleday, 1970), p. 139.
20. *Ibid.,* p. 192.
21. *Time* magazine (6 August, 1973), p. 54.

He spent time in Asia with various gurus, including the Tibetan Dalai Lama. Merton gave the closing address to the Conference in Calcutta on October 23, 1968. He told the assembly:

> If [all] are faithful to their own calling...and to their own message from God, communication on the deepest level is possible...Not that we discover a new unity. We discover an older unity. My dear brothers, we are already one. But we imagine that we are not. And what we have to recover is our original unity. What we have to be is what we are.[22]

His audience was largely composed of non-Christians from all over the world. What did he suggest in saying: "My dear brothers, we are already one"? We are left to figure out whether he had joined his hearers or whether his hearers had joined him. Just before his accidental death in Bangkok, on December 10, 1968, he told a gathering of Christian monks and nuns from various parts of Asia: "The monk is a man who has attained or is about to attain, or seeks to attain, full realization. He dwells in the center of society as one who has attained realization—he knows the score."[23]

Time magazine (August 6, 1973) reported that "his death prompted friends to speculate whether Merton would ever have returned to the U.S. from his enthusiastic plunge into Buddhism. The answer now seems to be yes, though he might not have returned to Gethsemani itself."

Some Buddhists revere Merton as a reincarnated Buddha, while one spirit medium reports that Merton has escaped the cycle of reincarnation and is now the Ascended Master "Davog," whose task is to prepare for the Second Coming of Jesus.[24]

---

22. William H. Shannon, *Thomas Merton's Dark Path: The Inner Experience of a Contemplative* (New York: Farrar, Straus & Giroux, 1981), p. 215.
23. Shannon, *Thomas Merton's Dark Path*, p. 216.
24. Edward Rice, *The Man in the Sycamore Tree*, pp. 11, 139.

Doubtless, Merton was remarkable. Anyone who captured such interest from Christians, Eastern mystics and occultists would have to be. It is regrettable that he found traditional Christianity so insufficient (and even maddening), feeling instead the need to look to the East for truth.

Some individuals have dabbled ignorantly in Eastern religion. Others are fully aware of what they do. Priests and nuns are teaching Hindu meditation. An American archbishop reportedly does Yoga.[25] Thousands of Catholics have been introduced to spirit guides and visualization techniques. They are in danger. They need our prayers.

25. Leon V. King, *The Wanderer,* "Why Rembert Ate Meat," 22 January, 1987.

4.

Pierre Teilhard de Chardin

In 1980, Marilyn Ferguson published her book, *The Aquarian Conspiracy: Personal and Social Transformation in the 1980's*. In it, she favorably describes the New Age Movement as:

> A leaderless but powerful network...working to bring about radical change in the United States. Its members have broken with certain key elements of Western thought, and they may even have broken continuity with history.[1]

She describes how new ideas are changing people everywhere: in business, religion, leisure and sports. Ferguson writes:

> It seems to speak to something very old. And perhaps, by integrating magic and science, art and technology, it will succeed where all the king's horses and all the king's men failed.
>
> The transformative process, however alien it may seem at first, soon feels irrevocably right. Whatever the initial misgivings, there is no question of commitment

---

1. Marilyn Ferguson, *The Aquarian Conspiracy: Personal and Social Transformation in the 1980's* (Los Angeles: J.P. Tarcher, 1980), p. 23.

once we have touched something we thought forever lost—our way home. Once this journey has begun in earnest, there is nothing that can dissuade. No political movement, no organized religion commands a greater loyalty.[2]

The Hinduistic flavor of much New Age religion is not innately attractive to the Western mind. Its emphasis upon the illusory nature of matter does not come naturally to many of us. The materialism of our society could be a roadblock to the popularity of the New Age Movement, were it not for the writings of the French Jesuit priest, Pierre Teilhard de Chardin.

It is Teilhard whose work has glorified, rather than denied, the material world. For him, matter is sacred; he made the idea of the "God within" work. Teilhard theorized a synthesis of the spiritual and the material which has had a conspicuous effect not only on many Catholics, but upon "Aquarian Conspirators" everywhere.

In her book, Marilyn Ferguson published a survey of persons involved in "social transformation." These self-proclaimed "conspirators" singled out one man more often than any other. Pierre Teilhard de Chardin was the individual most frequently cited as having had a profound influence upon their thinking. The list headed by Teilhard included a wide range of influential figures including C.G. Jung, Aldous Huxley, Swami Muktananda, Thomas Merton, Buckminster Fuller, Werner Erhard and Maharishi Mahesh Yogi.[3]

It is my intention to shine a critical light on this deceased Jesuit priest's influential teachings and ideas. My hope is that others will be warned away from the real but false appeal contained in his theories.

---

2. *Ibid.*, pp. 18, 34.
3. *Ibid.*, p. 420.

Teilhard and Modernism

In 1903, Pierre Teilhard de Chardin was twenty-two years old and studying for the priesthood when Joseph Sarto, Patriarch of Venice, was elected Pope Pius X. Although Teilhard was too young to come under the scrutiny of Rome at the time of the publication of Pius X's encyclical "On Modernism" *(Pascendi),* he learned well the defensive techniques of his Modernist heroes, for he would use the same hypocritical tactics later during his own difficulties.

Representative of the Modernists' strategy is the case of the French priest, L'Abbé Alfred Loisy. Loisy popularized Modernist beliefs which he had imported from the Protestant liberal theologians of nineteenth-century Germany. Notable was his denial of the divinity of Jesus. Michael Davies, in his book, *Partisans of Error,* wrote of Loisy's relationship with and attitudes toward the Church and his superiors:

> St. Pius X had five of Loisy's books placed on the Index in December 1903. Loisy made a reluctant act of submission in 1904, but it was in no way sincere. He wrote in his journal for 10 May 1904: "I remain in the Church for reasons which are not of faith but of moral expediency."
>
> In a letter to Cardinal Merry del Val on 24 January 1904 he stated: "I accept all the dogmas of the Church."...His real thoughts were set down in his diary: "I have not been a Catholic in the official sense of the word for a long time...Roman Catholicism as such is destined to perish, and it will deserve no regrets." In an entry dated 12 May 1904 he states: "Pius X, the head of the Catholic Church, would excommunicate me most decidedly if he knew that I hold...the virgin birth and the resurrection to be purely moral symbols, and the entire Catholic system to be a tyranny which acts in the name of God and Christ against God himself and against the Gospel." Despite all the incontrovertible evidence which proves the insincerity of Loisy and other Modernists, they still have apologists

today who depict them as sincere and selfless seekers after truth, noble scholars who fell victim to an ignorant and unscrupulous clerical bureaucracy. In the Liberal Catholic mythology, Loisy is still the hero and St. Pius X the villain.[4]

Pius X understood the Modernists' attitude toward the Church's rejection of their teachings. Some excerpts from *Pascendi:*

> The Modernists express astonishment when they are reprimanded or punished. What is imputed to them as a fault they regard as a sacred duty. For them to speak and to write publicly is their bounden duty. Let authority rebuke them as much as it pleases—they have their own consciences on their side and an intimate experience which tells them with certainty that what they deserve is not blame but praise.
>
> They go their way, reprimands and condemnations not withstanding, masking an incredible audacity under a mock semblance of humility. While they make a show of bowing their heads, their hands and minds are more boldly intent than ever on carrying out their purposes.
>
> And this policy they follow willingly and wittingly, both because it is part of their system that authority is to be stimulated but not dethroned, and because it is necessary for them to remain within the ranks of the Church in order that they may gradually transform the collective conscience.[5]

Teilhard de Chardin was teaching at the Catholic Institute in Paris when he first ran afoul of the Church's teachings. He wrote an essay, not intended for publication, for the purpose of explaining his views on the Fall and Original Sin. In it, he denied the existence of Adam, Eve, Paradise, or a time before man had sinned.

---

4. Michael Davies, *Partisans of Error: St. Pius X Against the Modernists* (Long Prairie, MN: The Neumann Press, 1983), pp. 70-71.
5. Pius X, *Pascendi Gregis* (London: Burns & Oates Ltd., 1907), pp. 33, 34.

Eventually Teilhard's essay came to the attention of Church authorities, who were forced to act, in view of his position as a teacher. Rome demanded that he give up his teaching position at the Institute and that he sign a statement reversing his earlier written position.

Ellen and Mary Lukas explain Teilhard's dilemma in their book, *Teilhard*. His friend and old classmate, Auguste Valensin, counseled him that:

> There is nothing he could do but yield entirely or leave. After considerable deliberation, Valensin decided that Teilhard's best course was to consider the physical action of signing the document as a gesture of fidelity rather than a symbol of intellectual assent, and sign it. Fundamentally, he argued all the Society asked for was obedience. Heaven would judge the rest.
>
> He...put his signature to every proposition Rome demanded—even though, as he wrote Edouard Le Roy, he had not changed his ideas or his sense of mission in the slightest.
>
> "I stand condemned," he once remarked..."by dolts and ignoramuses!"[6]

This was only the first encounter in a lifetime during which Teilhard's ideas would be repeatedly rejected. A rough chronology of his difficulties runs as follows:

1911: Pierre Teilhard is ordained a Jesuit priest.

1920: Teilhard teaches at the Institut Catholique in Paris.

1924: His initial troubles begin with his earlier written essay in which he denied the Fall of man, the existence of Adam and Eve and the Garden of Eden.

1925: Rome demands he give up his Institut teaching position and sign a retraction of his views. He signs.

---

6. Mary Lukas and Ellen Lukas, *Teilhard: The Man, The Priest, The Scientist* (Garden City, NY: Doubleday, 1977), pp. 94-95.

1927: Rome refuses to grant an Imprimatur to *The Divine Milieu*.

1933: Teilhard is ordered not to teach in Paris and is refused permission to publish his book, *Human Energy*.

1937: In May, Teilhard is "ordered by his major superiors to stop disseminating his outrageous ideas. . . ."

1944: His most famous work, the *Phenomenon of Man,* is banned. He is refused professorship at College de France.

1947: *Phenomenon of Man* is extensively reworked in order to pass Church scrutiny. Instead, Rome forbids his writing or teaching on any but scientific subjects.

1948: *Phenomenon of Man* is again refused publication.

1949: Teilhard's printings and activities are restricted. He is refused permission to publish *The Human Zoologic Group*.

1951: Lives in U.S. until 1955.

1955: Printings and activities again restricted. Pierre Teilhard de Chardin died April 10, 1955.

1957: Holy Office decree ordering withdrawal of his works from Catholic libraries, religious institutions and bookstores.

1962: John XXIII issues a *monitum* (warning) against "serious errors" in Teilhard's works.

1981: *L'Osservatore Romano* states that the *monitum* is still in effect.

Teilhard's Theology

Teilhard believed in two kinds of energy inherent in all matter. First of all, there is *tangential* energy. Tangential energy is familiar because it so definitely surrounds us. It is physical energy, or what Teilhard would call external or "the without." Subject to *entropy,* tangential energy tends toward disorder or diffusion.

But Teilhard also theorized a second form of energy, which he called *radial* energy. This internal energy or "the within" might be called spiritual or psychic energy. Unlike tangential energy, radial energy tends toward complexity. It has purpose or consciousness, thus providing direction for its evolutionary course. In the beginning, the extremely simple consciousness of elemental matter was supposedly sufficient to cause the formation of more complex molecules. This resulting increase of complexity led in turn to a higher level of consciousness. This cycle of consciousness—complexity—higher consciousness—higher complexity—is Teilhard's mechanism for evolution.

He seems to suggest that this radial energy or consciousness can be equated with God. It is true that God holds all the universe in existence at all times, for, as St. Paul says, "in him we live, and move, and have our being." (*Acts* 17:28). (But it is *wrong* to say that God is "immanent," for immanent means to *be* or to *be identical with* His creation. The fallacy of saying God is immanent is that He is thereby said to be identical with His creation, which is finite; and therefore God would be finite instead of infinite, which is obviously false.) Therefore, to deny that God is transcendent or existing independent of His creation is to say that He is no God at all. Teilhard's God has existence only in matter, for without matter He could not exist. Teilhard wrote in *Human Energy:*

> One is inseparable from the other; one is never without the other...No spirit (not even God within the limits of our experience) exists, nor could structurally exist without an associated multiple, any more than a center without its circle or circumference. In a concrete sense there is not matter and spirit. All that exists is matter becoming spirit.

So much matter is needed for so much spirit.[7]

According to Teilhard, we are locked into a self-creating system in which matter will ultimately become spirit when the necessary level of both complexity and consciousness have been attained. This increasing "complexity-consciousness" is an upward spiral which has experienced several breakthroughs. This progression—from Pre-Life to Life, from Life to Thought—is to continue to the next stage: that of a superconsciousness where the radial energies of all mankind coalesce into a collective human organism stretched over the entire planet.

New Agers are eagerly awaiting this next step, but feel that it can only come about when a certain critical number of individuals are joined together to bring it about. Teilhard called it the Omega Point. Just like a nuclear chain reaction which can occur only when a certain critical mass of uranium or plutonium is brought together, the jump to Omega will occur only when a critical mass of humanity is ready. This excerpt from Ken Keyes' *The Hundredth Monkey* explains the New Agers' hope:

> The Japanese monkey, *Macaca fuscata*, has been observed in the wild for a period of over thirty years. In 1952, on the island of Koshima, scientists were providing monkeys with sweet potatoes dropped in the sand. The monkeys liked the taste of the raw sweet potatoes, but they found the dirt unpleasant.
>
> An 18-month-old female named Imo found she could solve the problem by washing the potatoes in a nearby stream. She taught this trick to her mother. Her playmates also learned this new way and they taught their mothers too. This cultural innovation was gradually picked up by various monkeys before the eyes of the scientists. Between 1952 and 1958 all the young mon-

---

7. Pierre Teilhard de Chardin, *Human Energy* (New York: Harcourt Brace Jovanovich, Inc., 1969), pp. 57, 162.

keys learned to wash the sandy sweet potatoes to make them more palatable. Only the adults who imitated their children learned this social improvement. Other adults kept eating dirty sweet potatoes.

Then something startling took place. In the autumn of 1958, a certain number of Koshima monkeys were washing sweet potatoes—the exact number is not known. Let us suppose that when the sun rose one morning there were 99 monkeys on Koshima Island who had learned to wash their sweet potatoes. Let's further suppose that later that morning the hundredth monkey learned to wash potatoes.

Then it happened! By that evening almost everyone in the tribe was washing sweet potatoes before eating them. The added energy of this hundredth monkey created an ideological breakthrough! But notice. A most surprising thing observed by these scientists was that the habit of washing sweet potatoes then jumped over the sea—colonies of monkeys on other islands and the mainland troop of monkeys at Takasakiyama began washing their sweet potatoes! Thus when a certain critical number achieves an awareness, this new awareness may be communicated from mind to mind.[8]

Whether this doubtful story is true or not, it perfectly illustrates the sort of wildfire shift in consciousness which Teilhard looks forward to. It also explains why we see the advocates of this sort of "super consciousness" getting together from time to time for "planetary healing meditations." They have done this over and over by now, each time without result. The reader may remember the Harmonic Convergence of August 16-17, 1987. Many of these New Age pilgrims traveled to various sacred planetary "pressure points," while the rest contented themselves with doing their treehugging, hand-holding, "ooommming" and "aahhhing" in local gatherings. If you do not remember this cosmic event,

8. Ken Keyes, Jr., *The Hundredth Monkey* (Coos Bay, Oregon: Vision Books, 1985), pp. 11-17.

it is probably because nothing happened except some muffled snickering. Lamented one frustrated advocate: "The media made us look like air-headed idiots."[9] Such failures do not, however, daunt the true believer. There is always next time. The hundredth monkey is out there somewhere. Meanwhile these exercises continue.

Sinful Rocks and Theosophist Roots

This system of Teilhard's is coherent. It holds together, but is it true? Teilhard was convinced that the destiny of matter would be fulfilled, but that individuals or civilizations could themselves fail to cooperate, thus delaying that destiny. It is a basic tenet of New Age thought that the only real sin is the refusal to live up to one's evolutionary duties and prepare for the inevitable future.

In this view it was not Satan or Adam and Eve who were the first sinners. Teilhard's ideas along this line are so comical that the reader will not believe me unless I quote: "We may say it is the characteristic of minerals (as of so many other organisms that have become incurably fixed) to have chosen a road which closed them prematurely in upon themselves."[10]

The first sinners were rocks, rocks who chose the wrong road. The good rocks were those early minerals who lived up to their duties and eventually became megamolecules capable of forming the variable patterns required to make the breakthrough from pre-life to life. Then there were those sinful rocks who merely formed crystals capable of growing only according to a set pattern. We are urged not to look back to earlier patterns, but instead to emulate those obedient

---

9. Cheryl Hoffman, "Planet Earth Energized by Harmonic Convergence," *The Standard*, Nov./Dec. 1987, p. 12
10. Pierre Teilhard de Chardin, *The Phenomenon of Man* (New York: Harper & Row, Harper Torchbook edition, 1965), p. 69.

forward-looking rocks by being open to the next step in our evolution.

Fr. Patrick O'Connell in his book, *Original Sin in the Light of Modern Science,* is right on the mark concerning Teilhard's ideas:

> In Father Teilhard's own country, France, prominent theologians, like Fr. Philip of the Trinity, O.C.D., one of the Consultors of Vatican II, has analyzed his religious writings and pointed out the grave errors against the faith which they contain, and prominent scientists like Professors Bounoure and Vernet of France have done the same for his scientific writings and have shown that he has no claim to be called a great scientist, or even to be called a scientist at all, but that he should rather be classified among the theosophists.[11]

The founding of the Theosophical Society in 1875 was contemporaneous with the rise of liberal Protestantism and "Catholic" Modernism. Helena Petrovna Blavatsky and Colonel Henry Olcott led the revival of what is called the Ancient Wisdom, an eclectic mix of Eastern mysticism, the Egyptian Mysteries, and Gnosticism, as well as elements from the writings of Plato, Plotinus and others. Evolution is a key doctrine. Dr. Douglas Baker, in his occult work, *Superconsciousness Through Meditation,* states:

> The first great postulate of Ancient Wisdom as set forth in *The Secret Doctrine* by Madame Blavatsky, is...the proposition that all things live. The tiniest atom is a sentinent [sic], living entity, as is the greatest galaxy in the heavens with its immense consciousness. Everything is alive: atoms are alive, minerals are alive, gemstones are alive.[12]

---

11. Rev. Patrick O'Connell, B.D., *Original Sin in the Light of Modern Science* (Houston, TX: Lumen Christi Press, 1973), p. 46.
12. Dr. Douglas Baker, *Superconsciousness Through Meditation* (New York: Samuel Weiser, Inc., 1978), p. 30.

One of the most important Theosophist offshoots was Alice A. Bailey's Lucis Trust, founded in 1922. In that year her first book, *Initiation, Human and Solar,* was published by her Lucifer Publishing Company. It has since changed its name to the more covert "Lucis Publishing Company." Her works were dictated to her telepathically by one of the so-called "Masters of Wisdom." It was these very ideas of the Theosophists which served as the seeds for the occultic, anti-Semitic foundations of Nazism. Theosophists and Nazis both employ the swastika as their emblem. In Alice Bailey's teachings she wrote in 1939 about "the Jewish problem," and later, after the horrors of "the Holocaust" were made public, she still maintained that "Orthodox Judaism, with its deep-seated hatred, must slowly disappear."[13]

Constance Cumbey, in her excellent book about the New Age Movement, *Hidden Dangers of the Rainbow,* writes:

> The writings of Alice Bailey, which have been followed meticulously by the New Age Movement, state that the new "messiah" will not be Jewish, as the Jews have forfeited that privilege, and that they must pass through the fires of purification in order to learn humility. (See *The Rays and the Initiations* by Alice A. Bailey. This particular passage regarding the New "Messiah" was written in 1949 when the entire world knew what had happened to Europe's Jewish population.) These teachings are also strongly opposed to "Zionism" and a possession of a homeland by the Jewish people. These teachings also state that what happened to the Jewish people in WW II was a result of their "bad national karma."[14]

The Alice Bailey writings call for a one-world government, a one-world leader called "the Christ," and a one-world reli-

---

13. Alice A. Bailey, *The Externalisation of the Hierarchy* (New York: Lucis Publishing Co., 1982), pp. 87, 543.
14. Constance E. Cumbey, *The Hidden Dangers of the Rainbow: The New Age Movement and our Coming Age of Barbarism* (Shreveport, LA: Huntington House, Inc., 1983), p. 115.

gion. It is not just the Jews who are a problem to them, because any monotheistic belief which depends upon a transcendent God is hateful to them. The same teachings are equally anti-Christian, and especially anti-Catholic. They speak of novel uses for atomic energy:

> The atomic bomb does not belong to the...nations who perfected it.... It belongs to the United Nations for use (or let us rather hope, simply for threatened use) when aggressive action...rears its ugly head. It does not essentially matter whether that aggression is the gesture of any particular nation or group of nations or whether it is generated by the political groups of any powerful religious organisation, such as the *Church of Rome, who as yet are unable to leave politics alone....*[15]

Teilhard's Social Theories

If Teilhard had not spelled out his vision for mankind, one might be tempted to speculate as to the nature of a society which is characterized by a single mind. As it is, Fr. Teilhard has made it very clear. In *Human Energy* he calls for a one-world government as the only answer to world problems: "The age of nations has passed. Now, unless we wish to perish we must shake off our old prejudices and build the earth."[16]

Fr. Teilhard has not left much to the imagination as to the form he foresees for this one-world government: "No serious progress can be made...except under two conditions: the first that the proposed organization must be international *and in the end totalitarian;* and secondly that it must be conceived on a very large scale."[17]

The editor of *Human Energy* adds a footnote to this passage apologizing for Teilhard's unfortunate use of the word

---

15. Alice A. Bailey, *The Externalisation of the Hierarchy,* p. 548 (emphasis added).
16. Pierre Teilhard de Chardin, *Human Energy,* p. 37.
17. *Ibid.,* p. 134 (emphasis added).

"totalitarian," saying that Teilhard meant to convey only a general notion of totality. In *The Future of Man,* Teilhard writes: "The modern totalitarian regimes, whatever their initial defects, are neither heresies nor biological regressions: They are in line with the essential trend of 'cosmic' movement."[18]

And who will rule in this glorious society? Obviously, Teilhard is not speaking of democracy or representative government, but of rule by an elite. The general population will not have a say in the future; rather:

> The world of tomorrow will be born out of the elected group of those (arising from any direction and class and confession in the human world) who will decide that there is something big waiting for us ahead, and give their life to reach it.[19]

This is not to contend that Teilhard envisioned a government that employs concentration camps and torture and murder, but what he does suggest can lead to little else. Teilhard appeals to something chillingly like the Nazi mentality of the 1930's or the ideas of the present-day euthanasia and abortion advocates. One wonders who would be the "useless eaters" in a Teilhardian society. He writes:

> The earth is a closed and limited surface. To what extent should it tolerate, racially or nationally, areas of lesser activity? More generally still, how should we judge the efforts we lavish on all kinds of hospitals on saving what is so often no more than life's rejects?
>
> To what extent should not the development of the strong (to the extent that we can define this quality) take precedence over the preservation of the weak? How can we reconcile, in a state of maximum efficiency, the care

---

18. Pierre Teilhard de Chardin, *The Future of Man* (New York: Harper & Row, 1969), p. 46.
19. Pierre Teilhard de Chardin, *Letters to Two Friends, 1926-1952* (New York: Meridian Books; World Publishing Co., 1969), p. 154.

lavished on the wounded with the more urgent necessities of battle?[20]

Once again his editor, attempting to mitigate such outrageous statements, notes that "Teilhard's constant efforts both to encourage the weak and inspire the strong prove that he knew how to make this reconciliation." Although the above quotations are couched as questions, terms such as "maximum efficiency" and "lavish efforts" would seem to prejudice the answer, especially when Teilhard continues the above discussion using worried references to the increasing scarcity of natural resources and how they might best be allocated. Even with the Nazi Holocaust fresh in his memory, Teilhard's naivete is incredible. Once in a debate on the subject of *Science and Rationality,* "he shocked his opponent by refusing to permit even the appalling evidence of the experiments of the doctors of Dachau to modify his faith in the inevitability of human progress. 'Man,' he asserted, 'to become fully man, must have tried everything. . . .' "[21]

Apparently, for Teilhard, evil is a necessary part of our evolution. But further, we cannot become "fully man" until we have committed every conceivable atrocity.

What are we to make of Teilhard's visions of a one-world, elitist, totalitarian government? Where should we stand on his theology which speaks little of Christ, nearly nothing of Jesus and squares best with the teachings of occultists bent upon the destruction of Christianity? One can understand why he is the patron saint of New Agers, but then cultists and occultists have played at least a small part in every age, so why sound an alarm now? Since his death, Teilhard has become an increasingly fashionable figure among Catholics, even though the monitum of Pope John XIII condemning his works has never been revoked.

His writings have been translated into nearly every impor-

---

20. Pierre Teilhard de Chardin, *Human Energy,* pp. 132-133.
21. Mary Lukas and Ellen Lukas, *Teilhard,* pp. 237-238.

tant language and the copies number in the many millions. His devotées include Assistant Secretary General of the United Nations, Robert Muller. Muller, who claims to be a Roman Catholic, described his "Five Teilhardian Enlightenments" in his book, *New Genesis.* One of the best-known "Teilhardians" is New York Governor Mario Cuomo. Joseph Sobran, in the *National Right to Life News* (1/10/85), reported:

> Cuomo has spoken freely of his discovery of the writings of Teilhard de Chardin, the Jesuit theologian who fashioned a "scientific" yet mystical version of Catholicism for people who don't like Catholicism. Cuomo credits Teilhard's vision with making his own faith less rigid, more "humane." So he has apparently undergone some sort of inner conversion.[22]

Undoubtedly, many people are attracted to Teilhard because of his promise of inevitable progress for humanity. He offers a way out of our present predicament. But it is apparent that many are grossly naive about certain of his political theories. In the March 30, 1985 issue of *America,* Thomas M. King quotes Governor Cuomo's comments concerning Teilhard's political agenda:

> Perhaps the ideal is vague, but Teilhard never spelled out his politics. It is not easy to say what he would recommend in today's political world, but he would insist that we look beyond the differences that divide us and develop a sense of our common humanity. And he would also insist that such work is holy—for those who have the eyes to see.[23]

In his speech accepting the Democratic vice-presidential nomination in 1972, Sargent Shriver made reference to Teilhard. Teilhard has also been very well-received by Marxists,

---

22. Joseph Sobran, "Mario Cuomo and the Anti-Church," *National Right to Life News,* 10 January 1985.
23. Thomas M. King, "The Milieux Teilhard Left Behind," *America,* 30 March 1985, p. 252.

and even the Soviet Union has published a limited edition of *The Phenomenon of Man,* with numerous passages omitted.[24]

Fewer and fewer American Catholic publications are shy about quoting Teilhard glowingly. The *Catholic Update* turned its 1983 Christmas issue into a plug for New-Age-style activism. Writing about the New Creation, "We have only to believe," adds Teilhard de Chardin in *The Divine Milieu,* "then little by little, we shall see the universal horror unbend, and then smile upon us, and then take us in its more than human arms."[25]

Whatever it may mean to one day find ourselves in the inhuman arms of a grinning universal horror, one thing is clear: the acceptance of the ideas of Pierre Teilhard de Chardin by Catholics is becoming a *fait accompli.*

All this is not to say that Teilhard has not composed occasional snippets that might be taken for orthodoxy. Certainly, though, those are not the passages which endear him to the New Agers. On the other hand, such passages provide his defenders with a few phrases with which to reassure Catholics who find him suspect.

The writer of the article on Teilhard in the *New Catholic Encyclopedia* (1967) seems to bend over backwards in what is essentially a whitewash. The writer concedes that the Church has officially warned "against uncritical acceptance of his theories," but points out that the Church does not "question the value of his scientific work, or the righteousness of his intentions and the sincerity or fervor of his spiritual life." Of course, Teilhard is long dead and no one cares so much as a crumb about his science, his intentions or his sincerity. It is his *theories* that are embraced by the New Agers and questioned by the Church.

---

24. *Ibid.,* p. 252.
25. Carol Luebering, *Catholic Update* (Cincinnati, OH: St. Anthony Messenger Press, 1983), p. 4.

Teilhardism is deadly. To such ideas, the door of the Church has always been barred—barred to spiritualists, barred to witchcraft and barred to the lie of the "god within." Today, while we face a world of extreme physical danger, the greater danger is spiritual, and Teilhard has unbarred the door. The Christian needs discernment and, increasingly, courage, remembering that:

> For there shall be a time, when they will not endure sound doctrine; but, according to their own desires, they will heap to themselves teachers, having itching ears: and will indeed turn away their hearing from the truth, but will be turned into fables.
>
> (*2 Tim.* 4:3-4).

5.

The New Age Mystic: Different Path, Same God?

That Eastern concepts have pervaded much of the West should be apparent to all but the most superficial observer. We have holistic health and holistic medicine. Transcendental Meditation and other mind-control courses are multi-million-dollar businesses. Due to the popularity of Shirley MacLaine's "mystical" books and her movie, *Out on a Limb,* Americans are becoming increasingly familiar with altered states of consciousness, past lives and reincarnation, and contact with spirits through "trance channelers."

It comes, then, as no surprise that the Church has felt a tug toward the East. There is a Catholic magazine called *Praying: Spirituality for Everyday Living.* The articles are, of course, concerned with prayer, but unfortunately the emphasis is on New Age forms of prayer. One feature in the May-June, 1987 issue was a humorous piece showing ten cartoons depicting various prayer types. Seven of the ten dealt with Oriental or occult techniques.[1]

Since the 1960's there has occurred a surge of popularity

---

1. Kathleen Hightower, "Favorite New Ways to Pray," *Praying: Spirituality for Everyday Living,* May-June 1987, p. 17.

in what is billed as the "revival of ancient Christian prayer" techniques. These techniques are so nearly identical to Eastern (or "pagan") meditative systems that the proponents of these methods generally feel compelled to make some apology in order to answer the objections of the uninitiated.

Typically, the argument develops one of two possible lines of defense. The more orthodox meditator will insist that what he is doing is in some way essentially different from Hindu meditation and is therefore "Catholic." The second sort is far more bold and even arrogant. He doesn't care that the only thing Christian in his prayer is the name he gives it. His belief is that all paths lead to God. But do they?

One Way to God?

Is the Christian path the only way to achieve eternal life with God? Or are other religions valid prescriptions for other peoples? Are Hinduism, Buddhism, Mormonism and African religions valid paths to God?

Let me be clear that when I speak of a Hindu, I mean one who practices orthodox Hindu religion. In the same way, a Mormon is one who follows the teachings of Joseph Smith and Brigham Young. If a person calls himself a Mormon, claims allegiance to Joseph Smith, but does not believe that God the Father is a flesh and blood man or that Jesus and Lucifer were brothers, then that person is not an orthodox Mormon. If, instead, he ignores these doctrines, and begins to believe that Jesus Christ is the only-begotten Son of God who came to die for his sins, but still calls himself a Mormon, then we would find it difficult to consider him still a Mormon. The question I am raising concerns not this fellow in the middle, or the man who dissents from his creed, but the true follower of other religions.

A child in a religion class once defined "faith" as believing in something that you know isn't true. I have a friend who once repeated to me the old saw that the reason he believed in God was that "people need to believe in something greater than themselves."

Some psychologists might agree that belief in God can be mentally healthful (although most would merely advise belief in oneself), but surely there can be only one valid reason for believing in *anything,* including belief in God. We believe in something because we think it true.

This may seem obvious, but to a New Ager nothing is objectively true. What is truth for me may not be truth to him. He would say it is *my* truth, not *his.* You may recall that Our Lord once had a discussion with this sort of person:

> Pilate therefore said to him, Art thou a king then? Jesus answered: Thou sayest that I am a king. For this was I born, and for this came I into the world; that I should give testimony to the truth. Every one who is of the truth, heareth my voice. Pilate saith to him, What is truth? (*John* 18:37-38).

Good question—if you are genuinely interested in the answer! Some today are still asking this question. Some would claim that non-Christian religions are legitimate alternate pathways to "the divine." Some people say that if Hindus worship the same God as the Christians, then maybe they have something to teach us. But when Hinduism contradicts the Bible by teaching reincarnation and promising godhood for mankind, what shall we think? When Buddhism denies that Jesus is the one and only Christ, is it the Holy Spirit of God that inspires Buddhist doctrine? And if God's Spirit is not behind the pagan religions, then which spirit is?

Now someone might protest that there is much good to be learned from non-Christian religions and that we ought to be more open-minded. That pagan religions have some good in them is not only observably true, but one can go even further, saying that Satan himself has many "good" qualities. What we call evil started out as something good, but then it was twisted and perverted. C.S. Lewis wrote:

> Evil is a parasite, not an original thing. The powers which enable evil to carry on are powers given it by

goodness. All the things which enable a bad man to be effectively bad are in themselves good things— resolution, cleverness, good looks, existence itself.[2]

The mere fact that a religion holds to an attractive ethical system is nothing. The New Agers like to say that all truth is God's truth. That's right. But whatever good baggage they have collected along the way, they got it from Him. If it upholds beauty instead of ugliness, kindness over cruelty, what does this prove? It may only show another good trait of the devil, that is, his intelligence. If one wants to lure another into something harmful, then it would prove effective to paint a beautiful picture to trap the foolish. If a belief system is 99% true, but the remaining 1% is a fatal error, then it will serve the devil perfectly. "For Satan himself transformeth himself into an angel of light. Therefore it is no great thing if his ministers be transformed as the ministers of justice, whose end shall be according to their works." (*2 Cor.* 11:14,15).

As for selective obedience to the law of God, St. James says, "And whosoever shall keep the whole law, but offend in one point, is become guilty of all." (*James* 2:10). A footnote in the Bible (Douay-Rheims) explains that by committing even one mortal sin a person "despises the lawgiver. . . . For all the precepts of the law are to be considered as one total and entire law, and as it were a chain of precepts, where, by breaking one link of this chain, the whole chain is broken. . . ."

About Himself, Our Lord spoke, "I am the way, and the truth, and the life. No man cometh to the Father, but by me." (*John* 14:6). St. Paul says, "He that glorieth, may glory in the Lord. . . . For other foundation no man can lay, but that which is laid; which is Christ Jesus." (*1 Cor.* 1:31; 3:11). The Apostle goes much further in the same letter. After explaining the true way of salvation, he continues by distinguishing the Eucharist from pagan sacrifices:

---

2. C.S. Lewis, *Mere Christianity* (New York: Macmillan Publishing Co., 1979), p. 35.

But the things which the heathens sacrifice, they sacrifice to devils, and not to God. And I would not that you should be made partakers with devils. You cannot drink the chalice of devils: you cannot be partakers of the table of the Lord, and of the table of devils. (*1 Cor.* 10:20-21).

Such strong words are not easy to take.

It is easy to find individual Hindus who display more kindness or patience than some individual Christians. (But Christian virtues are shot through with charity, or love of God by grace, whereas Hindu virtues have a different generator and intention.) Many teachers are convinced that we have much to learn from the East, especially when Eastern meditation offers techniques and experiences which traditional Christianity apparently lacks. Does Oriental religion really offer value which Christianity does not?

Did the God who created the universe become a man and suffer a slow death by torture because Buddhism was already sufficient? Would not some other less drastic means have sufficed? If a Hindu guru has the answer, then Christianity is a cruel, inhuman hoax. No, we understand Christ's sacrifice and know that without His death and Resurrection we would still be "in our sins" (see *1 Cor.* 15:17) and barred from Heaven. God has left nothing we need out of the Church He founded 2,000 years ago.

Sadhana

Jesus Christ offered no *guaranteed techniques* for those seeking experiences of God. Both the Old Testament and New Testament speak of prayer as a communicating with God, rather than as the cultivation of an inner experience. Think of the Our Father, for example, which is a combination of praising God, submitting to His Will, and begging His pardon and help. The pattern Our Lord gave stands out in sharp contrast to Eastern methods:

When ye pray, you shall not be like the hypocrites, that love to stand and pray in the synagogues and corners of the streets, that they may be seen by men. Amen I say to you, they have received their reward. But thou when thou shalt pray, enter into thy chamber, and having shut the door, pray to thy Father in secret: and thy Father who seeth in secret will repay thee. And when you are praying, speak not much, as the heathens. For they think that in their much speaking they may be heard. Be not you therefore like to them, for your Father knoweth what is needful for you, before you ask him. Thus therefore shall you pray: Our Father who art in heaven, hallowed be thy name. (*Matt.* 6:5-9).

To be a Catholic means, among other things, to have a hunger for God. The yearning for Him is so strong that Christians, even though aware of their complete unworthiness, can have no greater pleasure than to have fellowship with Him, to enjoy Him. It is this desire that makes many people receptive to teachers who promise to "teach us to pray."

Let us explore the writings of one of these teachers to illustrate what has been passing for "spirituality" in the Church in recent years. I have not singled out this author/lecturer because he is alone in what he teaches or because he is the most "Eastern." He is merely representative.

Fr. Anthony de Mello

Fr. Anthony de Mello was a Jesuit from India. An internationally noted speaker until his sudden death in 1987, he led workshops on the subject of Eastern and Western prayer experiences and wrote the "How to do it" book: *Sadhana: A Way to God.* Subtitled "Christian Exercises in Eastern Form," *Sadhana* is published in the U.S. by The Institute of Jesuit Sources, St. Louis, Missouri. The cover of the book shows Jesus upon the Cross. At His feet sits a meditating figure, legs crossed in the traditional lotus position.

Sadhana's Foreword to the North American Edition suggests to the reader that trendy Catholics ought to jump onto the Eastern meditation bandwagon, or risk being left behind. After all, it must be good, considering how many important people are helping to drag this pagan idol into the church.

The 700,000 American practitioners of Transcendental Meditation (TM) are cited approvingly as one indication of the growing interest in Oriental religions and techniques for achieving the contemplative (read "altered") state of mind. It says that TM can be either Christian or Zen Buddhist prayer. Continuing, the Foreword cites Fr. William Johnston from his book, *The Still Point: Reflections on Zen and Christian Mysticism:*

> Not only Zen but all forms of Buddhism are going to make an enormous impact on the Christianity of the coming century...There is every likelihood that the future will see the rise of an Oriental Christianity in which the role of Buddhism will be incalculably profound. Indeed this process has already begun.[3]

Before giving instructions, Fr. de Mello gives two caveats. First, he explains that the reader will not master the material by reading it. It is necessary to "experience" the things taught. Secondly, he gives the first of several veiled warnings about possible dangers that could arise from the practice of his exercises.

The author takes the seeker through a number of exercises, beginning simply enough with the preparatory stage of stillness:

> Close your eyes once again. Get in touch with sensations...of your body...You will gradually feel a certain stillness in your body. Do not explicitly rest in the stillness.
>
> I repeat, do not explicitly rest in the stillness...If you do so, you run the danger of inducing a mild trance....[4]

3. Anthony de Mello, *Sadhana: A Way to God, Christian Exercises in Eastern Form* (St. Louis: The Institute of Jesuit Sources, 1978), p. x.
4. *Ibid.,* pp. 14, 15.

Soon, though, Fr. de Mello allows that if the stillness over-powers you, let go and surrender to it. Enjoy! Soon the novice learns that only through achieving altered states of conscious-ness is he able to understand reality. By the time the seeker reaches exercise number three, he has already learned reluc-tance to answer foolish questions about his experience. Fr. de Mello writes:

> What is the benefit of all this...? The only reply I shall give you for now is: Don't ask questions.
>
> You will also experience a disinclination to answer the questions, even seemingly practical questions, of others on these matters....The only worthy answer to them is, "Open your eyes and see for yourself."[5]

Before the novice can progress very far into the depths of the mind he must become the mind's master. A key to mind control is correct body posture. As in the traditional Hindu meditation, the most effective position is with the back and head erect. Fr. de Mello writes:

> The ideal posture for this is the lotus posture that stu-dents of yoga are taught: legs intertwined with feet rest-ing upon opposite thighs and spine erect. I am told that people who manage to attain this posture have such little difficulty with distractions that they actually have trou-ble thinking and getting their thinking mind to function at all.[6]

Once the mind and the posture are right, it is time for breathing exercises. The novice is to concentrate on the air flowing through the nostrils; its temperature, its volume. He is to keep his awareness on the breath for only ten to fifteen minutes. Fr. de Mello cautions against using this exercise for extended periods, at least not without a competent "guide." He mentions possible hallucinations from the practice, and

---

5. *Ibid.*, p. 16.
6. *Ibid.*, p. 20.

warns that it may dredge up unspecified "material" from the meditator's unconscious which he may find uncontrollable. The dangers are real, not only spiritually, but mentally as well. For a more forthright explanation of the "Perils of the Path," here are a few excerpts from the (non-Christian) book by Eknath Easwaran, *Meditation: Commonsense Directions For an Uncommon Life:*

> Please do not, in a burst of enthusiasm, increase your meditation to an hour or longer, because such a practice exposes you to dangers.
>
> What dangers?. . .a few [people] have an inborn capacity to plunge deeply inward. And once you break through the surface level, you are in an uncharted world. It is like a desert, but instead of sand there are latent psychological tendencies, terribly powerful forces. There you stand in that vast desert without a compass. You have tapped forces before you are prepared to handle them, and your daily life can be adversely affected by them.
>
> You may see lights, perhaps brilliant ones, or hear sounds.
>
> Entering deeper consciousness is like descending into a cave. There are bewitching experiences, and there can also be awesome, even disorienting ones.
>
> One last warning: please do not try to connect the passage to a physiological function, such as heartbeat or breathing rhythm. Such a connection may seem helpful initially, but it can cause serious problems later. Trying to synchronize your mantram with physiological processes, such as heartbeat or breathing, also divides your attention. No harm will result if this happens by itself, but do not try to make the connection. Actually, it can be quite hazardous to interfere with vital functions that are already operating smoothly without our conscious intervention.[7]

---

7. Eknath Easwaran, *Meditation: Commonsense Directions for an Uncommon Life* (Petaluma, CA: Nilgiri Press, 1978), pp. 43, 53, 54, 71.

What is being implied here? That one can kill himself doing Yoga? Understandably, modern writers hoping to promote the practice are loath to dwell on the subject, but ancient Yoga texts are more forthright. The writer of the *Hatha Yoga Pradipika* warns "the breath is controlled by slow degrees, otherwise [by being hasty or using too much force] it *kills the practicer himself.*"[8]

It is impossible to read very much about meditation without receiving such warnings. Even openly Luciferic publications contain dark admonishments against "opening doors on to the astral plane which the student may have difficulty in closing."[9]

Hopefully, these red flags may tend to warn off some potential seekers. The authors of meditation guides advise exercising extreme caution unless accompanied by a "competent guide." Such books would perform a more valuable service if they plainly warned against monkeying around with these practices at all.

In *Sadhana* we are told, "Our Hindu masters in India have a saying: One thorn is removed by another. By this they mean that you will be wise to use one thought to rid yourself of all the other thoughts...The mind must have something to occupy it...an ejaculation that you keep repeating ceaselessly to prevent the mind from wandering...One thorn is just as good as another."[10] Later, though, Fr. de Mello adds that, when engaged in group chanting, the Sanskrit word OM is a great help. Also helpful is the regular striking of "a pleasant sounding gong."[11]

The mantra has a place in most of the popular Eastern-oriented systems. Some writers emphasize it more than others. Some, trying to seem less pagan, will advise using

8. *Hatha Yoga Pradipika,* p. 15 (emphasis added).
9. Alice A. Bailey, *Externalisation of the Hierarchy* (New York: Lucis Publishing Co., 1982), p. 18.
10. Anthony de Mello, *Sadhana,* pp. 28-29.
11. *Ibid.,* p. 45.

it only as often as needed to drive out distractions. For some meditators this means constant repetition, while for more adept "contemplatives" the altered state of mind is maintained with minimal use of the mantra.

The mantra may be any sound, although certain sounds are considered more effective for particular purposes. OM is considered especially powerful. While it may or may not have meaning for the meditator, the mantra should consist of a single word. Whole sentences or Scripture verses—which, incidentally, might be meditated on to very worthwhile ends—are not usually advised because they might provoke thoughts. The Catholic seeker is often advised to use a "Christian" mantra, such as:

> Jesus . . . Jesus . . . Jesus . . . Jesus . . . Jesus . . . Jesus
> . . . Jesus . . . Jesus . . . Jesus . . . Jesus . . . Jesus . . .
> Jesus . . . Jesus . . . Jesus . . . Jesus . . . Jesus . . . Jesus

It would seem that the thrust is to "baptize" non-Christian behavior with sacred trappings in order to make them acceptable to Christians. Occult practices cannot be so sanctified, but rather the Holy Name is profaned instead. Also, how many times can one repeat thoughtlessly any single word without recalling the command of Jesus quoted above when He forbade praying with vain repetitions. (This is not to say anything against repeating the Holy Name of Jesus as a prayer, directing our words with love to the Person we are addressing.)

It is reminiscent of the triumph of Elias over the Prophets of Baal (*3 Kgs.* 18). Elias challenged the Baal worshippers, pitting the God of Israel against the pagan god. Attempting to call down fire from heaven, the heathens repeated endlessly, from morning till noon: "O Baal, hear us! O Baal, hear us! O Baal!" etc. . .Well, they worked up quite a lather dancing and chanting and slashing themselves with swords, but they got nothing but taunts from Elias for their efforts. Contrast this with Elias' brief prayer:

> Lord, God of Abraham, and Isaac, and Israel, show this day that thou art the God of Israel, and I thy servant, and that according to thy commandment I have done all these things. Hear me, O Lord, hear me: that this people may learn that thou art the Lord God, and that thou hast turned their heart again. Then the fire of the Lord fell. (*3 Kgs.* 18:36-38).

Now that's effective prayer!

This is not to say that repeating a mantra is not effective at inducing the thoughtless state of mind. In fact, this is the chief defense made by the typical Christian guru against charges of "multiplying words as the Gentiles do." He answers that the "prayer word" is used to facilitate union with the Lord. In other words, it works, so how can it be "vain"?[12]

What Is the Difference, Anyway?

It is important to distinguish further between occult meditation, which is the foundation of all New Age beliefs, and Christian meditation, which is basic to true spiritual growth. First, what New Agers call meditation is nothing like *Christian* meditation. Meditative (or discursive mental) prayer, for the Christian, consists of a rational examination of God's truths, commands, mysteries or events from Holy Scripture, joined to activity of the heart in forming holy affections and resolutions. Notice how the Psalmist refers to meditation:

> I will *meditate* on thy commandments, and I will consider thy ways.

> Make me to understand the way of thy justifications, and I shall be exercised in thy wondrous deeds.

> I have understood more than all my teachers: because thy testimonies are my *meditation*. (*Psalm* 118:15,27,99).

---

12. M. Basil Pennington, O.C.S.O., *Centering Prayer: Renewing an Ancient Christian Prayer Form* (Garden City, NY: Doubleday & Co., 1980), p. 200.

> O how have I loved thy law, O Lord! it is my meditation all the day. (*Psalm* 118:97).

> Blessed is the man whose...will is in the law of the Lord, and on his law he shall meditate day and night. (*Psalm* 1:1, 2).

Beyond meditative prayer, there is the genuine mystical experience of *contemplation*. Contemplation is the absorption of the soul into a partial "vision" of God—an infused, loving knowledge of God. Although one can *prepare* for contemplation, it is a gift God gives *as He wills*. Neither Christian preparations nor the mindless techniques of bearded gurus have power to produce this infused knowledge of God. Yet here, at the level of such a towering gift, Satan best earns his title, "the ape of God." As a gift independent of discursive reason, contemplation can be open to counterfeiting by the devil. The Catholic tradition is one of caution and the need for proper spiritual direction and the discernment of a good director. Otherwise, we are easily fooled by the fraudulent offerings of spiritual quacks in their imitation of contemplation.

Unlike occult meditation, *whose goal is an opened and emptied mind,* Christian prayer has God as its object. The object of occult meditation is to make the mind an empty and open receptacle. This emptying of the mind and inversion into self causes one to gaze at nothing and wait for what he does not know. This should be contrasted with the Christian at prayer: he knows his object and turns toward God, not self. He is not seeking the glory of the god within, but the magnificent goodness of the transcendent God. The meditator is intent upon God and His Word—not as a means to an end, but as the end itself.

Occult meditation strives toward realization of oneness with the universe or ultimate reality or whatever it calls its god. The ultimate goal of Eastern meditation is to lose oneself in "the one," which means this big divine universe. There's no god out there except the universe itself, and our job is to lose our separate identities and blend in with the divine "oneness"—or rather, to come to realize that we already *are* just an aspect of the divine oneness.

The Catholic, too, wants union with God, but he knows that God is God and creatures are creatures. God has given all of us our own separate existence and He will never take it away. Through Sanctifying Grace, an amazing unity is brought about between the Creator and the creature. The Three Divine Persons dwell in us and impart to us a share in Their own divine life. God even makes us, as the Mass says, "partakers of His divinity." Yet this "must not be conceived in the pantheistic sense of the transformation of the soul into the Divinity: the infinite distance between Creator and created remains."[13]

The goal of our entire life in general and of our prayer in particular should be to receive "more and more" Sanctifying Grace, Divine Life, so as to be united as closely as possible, in our actions and in our very souls, with God who is All-Good, All-Knowing, All-Powerful and All-Holy. There is no comparison between this sublime end and some absorption into "oneness with the one" without caring whether we are being united with good or evil, wisdom or stupidity, power or impotence, purity or filth. This union with God through Sanctifying Grace is a beginning of the eternal life of Heaven, where "eye hath not seen, nor ear heard, neither hath it entered into the heart of man, what things God hath prepared for them that love him." (*1 Cor.* 2:9). This picture of eternity is given us in Revelation:

> Behold the tabernacle of God with men, and he will dwell with them. And they shall be his people; and God himself with them shall be their God. And God shall wipe away all tears from their eyes: and death shall be no more, nor mourning, nor crying, nor sorrow any more, for the former things are passed away. (*Apoc.* 21:3-4).

---

13. Ludwig Ott, *Fundamentals of Catholic Dogma*, p. 256.

It is impossible to reconcile these Eastern teachings and practices with either the Bible or the traditions of the Church. Catholic Tradition consists of the teachings of Christ to the Apostles handed down through time within the Mystical Body of Christ.

What is so amazing is that these New Age gurus feel it is their position, even their duty, to single-handedly enrich our Christian Tradition. In this way, their definition of tradition justifies the Eastern embellishments. One popular teacher writes:

> This gift of life has been handed on through the ensuing centuries, sixteen or so, till it has come down to us today. In our time it has been gifted with a new name, Centering Prayer, and a new packaging, the impress of our hands as we pass it on to other, younger eager minds and hearts. They too, as they receive it, mold it and, we hope, will pass it on in a fruitful and life-giving way. . . . I have not separated East from West, for, as I have indicated, the Jesus Prayer in its purest form is but another expression of the same tradition springing from the same source.[14]

Unfortunately, the "development of tradition" is used as an excuse for meddling beyond the limits of true Christian Tradition and into areas where Scripture has warned us away.

Another aid to successful meditation that Fr. de Mello suggests is to have the correct location for meditation. It is a common occult/Eastern belief that places have their own vibrations. Good "vibes" enhance meditations and bad "vibes" inhibit them. He recommends

> You make your contemplation each time in the same place, the same corner, a corner or a room that is reserved for this purpose only. . . . It helps to pray in "sacred" places that have been sanctified by the frequent practice of contemplation.[15]

---

14. M. Basil Pennington, O.C.S.O., *Centering Prayer,* p. 22.
15. Anthony de Mello, *Sadhana,* p. 55.

Fr. Basil Pennington, the father of modern "centering prayer" and an admirer of Anthony de Mello, adds to the "vibrations" discussion:

> We in the West are not so sensitively aware of vibrations. Yet they inevitably take their toll on us. A room that has been very full of busy activity or loud, hard music carries its charge long after. It is well to be aware of this when we have a choice of places to meditate.[16]

This concept of vibrations is purely an Eastern/occult idea; it is not of Christian origin. In comparing the way of Sadhana to the techniques of occultist meditation one must look very hard to find any differences. Most methods will advise reserving a room (or at least a corner) for meditation. It is to be used for no other purpose. Gradually the room or corner becomes "sacred." Some say it helps to have a picture of your favorite mystic hanging on the wall somewhere.[17]

Visualization and Spirit Guides

When I was nineteen years old I had the unfortunate experience of spending some time with a fellow who introduced me to the concept of visualization. Bob was ten years older than my friends and I. When he moved into our small town and opened up what was called a "head shop," many local teens, including myself, were drawn to this peculiar stranger. He was different from most other 30-year-olds and seemed to enjoy our "hanging out" at his shop, as well as joining us at our weekend parties. Bob's hair was long and over his ears, as was common at the time, a fact which made it all the more eerie when I saw an oil portrait of him in his home. In this painting his hair was pulled back, and I remember wondering to myself why anyone would want to portray himself with pointed ears like the devil.

---

16. M. Basil Pennington, *Centering Prayer,* p. 4.
17. Eknath Easwaran, *Meditation,* p. 45.

One weekend evening, my friends and I were out talking with Bob in a quiet park. Only those in our small group were present, and Bob chose that night to reveal to us that he was a witch. He explained (and demonstrated) to us his use of hypnosis, an important part of his "craft." Most important, though, and the real source of his power, he told us, was the technique of visualization.

"I killed a man once," he said. Everyone squirmed at his statement, but not one of us said a word in the darkness. Bob sensed our discomfort and explained:

> He was very bad and deserved to die. I would never use my power for evil purposes. The way I did it was like this: I sat on the floor in my room with my feet facing this guy's house. Then I went into a trance and began to visualize, over and over, this man having his brains beaten out with a hammer. I just kept that picture happening in my mind again and again.
>
> That night while driving, he lost control of his car on a curve. He was thrown out and had his skull crushed on the pavement.

It was a sobering and disquieting story to hear. I and most of my friends stayed away from Bob after that. That brief association with this self-proclaimed witch still makes me shudder, and I thank God for pulling me away from him, even at a time when God did not seem so important in my life.

It was this story which came back to my mind as I began to study the New Age Movement. Without any doubt, visualization is the foundation and basis for witchcraft, so-called "mind powers," and pagan shamanism. It is found in African and Native American religion in the practice of the witch doctor or medicine man.

Visualization is the attempt to manipulate the physical world or contact the spirit world by use of the imagination. Fr. Anthony de Mello, in *Sadhana,* teaches visualization as a technique for contacting Jesus:

> Imagine you see Jesus sitting close to you....
>
> Now speak to Jesus....If no one is around, speak out in a soft voice.
>
> Listen to what Jesus says to you in reply...or what you imagine him to say.
>
> People sometimes ask me how they can meet the Risen Lord in their lives. I know of no better way to suggest to them than this one.[18]

In another exercise, he asks the meditator to pick a symbol for God. It may be anything, a flower or a star (since the symbol does not matter, presumably even a golden calf or a Swastika would do):

> Having chosen your symbol, stand reverently in front of it....Say something to it...
>
> Now imagine that it speaks back to you....What does it say?[19]

Getting the chance to meet Jesus Christ personally (short of Heaven) would seem to be appealing, but such efforts are not in accord with Scripture. Regarding this issue of seeing Jesus, compare the above exercises with these words penned by St. Peter:

> Whom having not seen, you love: in whom also now, though you see him not, you believe: and believing shall rejoice with joy unspeakable and glorified; receiving the end of your faith, even the salvation of your souls. (*1 Ptr.* 1:8-9).

What is going on when the Christian goes into the reaches of his mind to get in touch with God? What harm can come from it—and besides, if a vision you have helps, then doesn't that prove the validity of the experience? It is obvious that the *fact* of an experience is no proof it comes from a good

---

18. Anthony de Mello, *Sadhana,* pp. 72-73.
19. *Ibid.,* p. 80.

source. Just because the image speaks, that is no evidence God has been contacted. Anyone who finds himself able to "call up" God is either being fooled by his own imagination or, worse, is in touch with a deceiving spirit.

At other points Fr. de Mello directs the reader to visualize a meeting with an old hermit, or conversing with statues, and even one sick exercise where you see your own cold corpse turning blue and rotting as the decomposed flesh falls away.[20] Contrast these techniques with the sort of meditation defined in the Spiritual Exercises of St. Ignatius (from which de Mello claims to draw much inspiration):

> Meditation consists in calling to mind some dogmatic or moral truth and reflecting on or discussing this truth according to each one's capacity, so as to move the will and produce in us amendment.[21]

Similarities between the Ignatian exercises and *Sadhana* are few. While St. Ignatius' exercises do sometimes require the picturing of biblical scenes upon which the student meditates, these are exercises of the thinking mind. There is no altered state of consciousness by which the meditator empties himself and invites the "spirit" to speak to him.

Sadhana is clearly a different beast, one that correlates well with Eastern/occult sources and hardly at all with the Christian Tradition. Some of these exercises are merely strange, others are probably harmless, but many (such as recorded here) move into realms through which no human can safely travel.

Rewriting the Scriptures

Another recently popular technique is Ira Progoff's *Intensive Journal* method. In workshops, retreats and tape series,

20. Anthony de Mello, *Sadhana,* pp. 81, 92.
21. *Spiritual Exercises of St. Ignatius* (New York: Frederick Pustet & Co., 1914), p. 54.

Catholics and others are taught that keeping the journal will enhance their spirituality. Of course there is nothing wrong with recording and reflecting upon insights gained in one's spiritual life. The question is more about which religious insights will be reflected upon and from what source they will be gained. The assumption seems to be that our Scriptures are no longer relevant and that we can do better rewriting them based on our own life experiences and meditations.

Dr. Ira Progoff, psychotherapist, professor and author, studied with psychologist/occultist C. G. Jung and afterward with Zen master D. T. Suzuki. He clearly presents his journaling method in his book, *At a Journal Workshop*. The back dust jacket should be quite inviting for Roman Catholics. Among the glowing reviews is one by a Catholic university professor and another by a priest who calls Progoff's workshop "the greatest single breakthrough in my spiritual life. . . . I would like to see every pastoral person get a chance to experience this."[22]

Part of the journaling experience is called Twilight Imaging, done in what Progoff calls an "intermediate state of consciousness" somewhere between sleep and waking. In this altered state we "behold" inward "perceptions" which present themselves unasked for.[23] In another lesson the image gets clearer with an exercise which is wholly occult and nearly indistinguishable from the spirit guide exercises of the Silva Mind Control method.

The "Inner Wisdom Dialogue" begins with the student entering the meditative state. A being chosen by the student arrives to impart the inner wisdom (although an unexpected figure may appear instead). Progoff narrates:

> We let our thoughts come to rest. Our breathing is slow. It becomes slower, softer. We are still.

---

22. Ira Progoff, *At a Journal Workshop* (New York: Dialogue House Library, 1975), dust jacket.

23. *Ibid.*, pp. 77-79.

> In the stillness we feel the presence of this person,
> this wisdom figure, this being.
>   They speak to us.
>   We speak and we are spoken to. And we let it be writ-
> ten through our pen.[24]

As usual, the communications are automatically assumed to be good. In time, the meditator can expect to make contact with a number of these spirit guides. With the classic spiritualistic device of dictating written material through a medium, the whole picture should be clear enough to warn off even the half-asleep Christian. Incredible as it may seem, though, "thousands of priests, nuns and lay people, as well as official Catholic 'spiritual renewal' institutions are enthusiastically embracing this method."[25] I have copies of the annual schedule for the Intensive Journal workshops and retreats. Recent years show *dozens* of Catholic retreat houses and colleges sponsoring the method each year.

One might think some of the advice as doled out by the visualized images would be questioned, but this is never given any serious thought. The opposite is actually the rule, because the experience is always considered self-authenticating. One writer explained why only good can come to those who open themselves up to this experiential religion. Although the excerpt below refers to "centering prayer," the author has admitted that the prayer experience produces the desire for closer contact with non-Christian practice:[26]

> We need have no fear of the deceptions of the Evil One,
> because he cannot touch us at that level of our being.
> He can only affect those images and feelings that are
> influenced through the body. He cannot himself pene-

---

24. *Ibid.,* pp. 281-284.
25. Ralph Martin, *A Crisis of Truth* (Ann Arbor, MI: Servant Books, 1982), p. 63.
26. M. Basil Pennington, "Centering Prayer," *America,* 28 February 1987, p. 171.

trate into our spiritual being. There is a danger...in active prayer, in which we are using our imagination and feelings, for he can influence these. But in Centering Prayer we ignore these faculties...so the Evil One cannot touch it. We are engaged at a level that the Lord has made his own....We are out of the Devil's reach. Only God can penetrate this level of our being. So we are completely safe...[27]

Thus everything is turned upside down. The danger is in our lowly bedtime prayers, because there we pray under the influence of our imaginations and tired bodies. But safety is in the brainless opening of an empty mind with solemn assurance that Satan cannot function in the spirit realm.

Is Satan really unable to "penetrate into our spiritual being"? If we mean, "Can he control our intellect and will?" then no, not unless we let him. Even the demoniacs of the New Testament were not acting out their own will, but rather that of the possessing demon. But that is no comfort when the victim's own will has voluntarily opened the door to the spirits. The simple fact that these practices appear to grease the skids for more advanced occult practices should warn us from taking even the first step. We must remember with whom we are dealing. It is St. Paul who reminds us that the spiritual realm is the devil's natural element:

> For our wrestling is not against flesh and blood; but against principalities and powers, against the rulers of the world of this darkness, against the spirits of wickedness in the high places. (*Eph.* 6:12).

May God keep safe the unwary souls who venture there.

---

27. M. Basil Pennington, *Centering Prayer,* pp. 191-192.

6.

Witchcraft, WomanChurch, and the Goddess

Fr. Matthew Fox

One of the most enigmatic spectacles in modern Catholic America is the popularity of Dominican priest Fr. Matthew Fox. His books, *Whee! We, wee* and *On Becoming a Musical, Mystical Bear* and *Original Blessing* (and others) can be found on the shelves of many Catholic as well as occultic bookstores.

As any Catholic knows, and as the Church teaches, there is a sin that is inherited from Adam and is only removed through Christ's redemption.[1] Scripture, too, is in exact agreement: "For as by the disobedience of one man, many were made sinners; so also by the obedience of one, many shall be made just." (*Romans* 5:19).

In *Original Blessing,* Fox denies the traditional doctrine of Original Sin. He says we do not enter existence as sinful creatures: "We burst into the world as 'Original Blessings.' " The only sin Fox recognizes is the sin of dualism, i.e., of seeing people and things as being separate from one another.

---

1. Ludwig Ott, *Fundamentals of Catholic Dogma*, p. 108.

The only sin is the refusal to see all as one.[2]

His brand of religion is aptly called "Creation-Centered Spirituality." Creation-Centered Spirituality is focused not on God the Creator, but on god the creation. Fr. Fox is calling for Catholics to be in the leadership of the new spiritual age based on Creation-Centered Spirituality.

In her book *A Planned Deception,* Constance Cumbey wrote a chapter entitled "The Incredible Heresies of Father Matthew Fox." She related her experience of hearing Matthew Fox address parish leaders in a talk sponsored by the Liturgy Committee of the Archdiocese of Detroit:

> He shamelessly committed public blasphemy against the Holy Spirit, by telling an impressionable audience well under the spell of his hypnotic powers that the Holy Spirit was demanding they adopt wicca (witchcraft), shamanism, and goddess worship. Hundreds of well-dressed parish leaders and nuns listened to him in trance-like rapture. They appeared to adore Matthew Fox! One distinguished-looking CCD teacher proudly told me that he had taught St. Thomas Aquinas and St. Augustine for 30 years. "That was," he said, "a waste of time. I wish I had been teaching Father Matthew Fox!"[3]

As with all true New Agers, Fox insists that sin consists in the failure to embrace the New Age, the Age of Aquarius. He warns in *Whee! We, wee All the Way Home...A Guide to a Sensual, Prophetic Spirituality:*

> One tradition that offers us a glimpse into our own futures...is the astrological tradition.
>
> In particular, Jung subscribes to the way of seeing human history in 2000-year stages corresponding to the Age of the Bull (4000-2000 B.C.), a symbol of primitive instinctual civilizations and represented by Cretan

---

2. Matthew Fox, O.P., *Original Blessing: A Primer in Creation Spirituality* (Santa Fe, NM: Bear & Company, Inc., 1983), pp. 47, 49.
3. Constance Cumbey, *A Planned Deception: The Staging of a New Age Messiah* (East Detroit, MI: Pointe Publishers, Inc., 1985), p. 133.

religion; the Age of the Ram (2000 B.C.-1 A.D.), characterized by the religions of the Jews and the emergence of conscience and awareness of evil wherein religion sacrificed rams; the Age of Pisces, the fishes (1 A.D.-1997 A.D.), dominated religiously by the figure of Christ. . . .

There is an extremely important Caveat and danger sign that looms on our journey. That is the warning not to look back. . . . If you recall, when Moses came down from his experience with God on the mountain top, he was so infuriated by what he saw the Israelites doing that he broke the commandment tablets. What were they doing? They were whoring after the past gods! They were worshipping the religion of the previous age, the Age of the Bull. They refused to face the new spiritual consciousness that Moses ushered in, that of the Age of the Ram.

So we, too, on the verge of breaking into a new spiritual age, need to beware of the Gods of the past. . . .We have a clear lesson from the Israelites: to look back piningly is to commit idolatry.[4]

What delusion is it that allows Catholics to believe teaching which insists that to remain within traditional, biblical Christianity is idolatry, that it is "whoring after past gods"? It seems impossible that anyone could be so deceived, but in his Second Letter to the Thessalonians, St. Paul wrote of how those who were headed for destruction would not turn aside from their chosen course:

> Because they receive not the love of the truth, that they might be saved. Therefore God shall send them the operation of error, to believe lying: that all may be judged who have not believed the truth, but have consented to iniquity. (*2 Thess.* 2:10-11).

4. Matthew Fox, *Whee! We, wee All the Way Home. . .A Guide to a Sensual, Prophetic Spirituality* (Santa Fe, NM: Bear & Company, Inc., 1981), pp. 30, 242.

Whereas Pierre Teilhard de Chardin bridges the gap between East and West, Matthew Fox champions the paganism of the West. Like Teilhard, he worships matter as his God, but Fox repudiates Teilhard for his belief in self-denial and renunciation of pleasure-seeking.[5] He believes that "enough evils and crosses exist in our lives without making up new ones."[6] Fox is perhaps the American Church's most enthusiastic cheerleader for hedonism or what he calls "ecstasy."

In the New Age Movement, drugs can be more than just a way to have fun and pass the time until "the Christ" comes. Drugs can play an important role in altering consciousness. Whether it is the LSD popularized in the 60's or the peyote of the Indian sorcerer in the Carlos Castaneda books, the use of drugs serves as a shortcut to "mystical" experience. The same occult meditative states that normally require extended practice to achieve are effortlessly attained through drug use. The same experiences and even the spirits encountered are common to both methods. In fairness, it must be said that most genuine gurus will snub the drug user's "training wheels" as an expedient which does not ultimately lead to the very highest (or lowest?) states.

In Fox's book, *On Becoming a Musical, Mystical Bear,* he has written that while "excess" drug use is not wise, "intelligent use of drugs" is unquestionably an aid to prayer. Its value, says Fox, is in opening up one's awareness and also as a temporary escape from the worries of the everyday world. He maintains that "drugs can democratize spirituality, which has for so long been imagined to be in the hands and hearts of the wealthy, leisurely classes."[7]

Before looking further into Fox's paganism, it is worth

5. *Ibid.,* pp. 217-218.
6. Matthew Fox, "Self-denial Can Make You Selfish," *U.S. Catholic,* February 1978, p. 37.
7. Matthew Fox, *On Becoming a Musical, Mystical Bear: Spirituality American Style* (New York: Paulist Press, 1976), pp. 125-27.

examining his view of Jesus Christ. In *Original Blessing,* Fr. Fox rates numerous historical figures on their *creation-centeredness.* On a scale of one to five, Our Lord gets a "five," but (as in the theology of Teilhard) He really has no place at all except as an example of a wise man among other wise men and women.[8] Fr. Fox says that Jesus *"was always looking for wisdom in order to grow in wisdom,"* and he refers to Jesus Christ as *"weak and imperfect."*[9] Rejecting the truth that Jesus Christ came to die for man's sins, Fox paints a picture not of Him embracing His Father's will, but as trying to escape the sacrifice of Calvary. Speaking of Our Lord facing the Crucifixion, Fr. Fox says, "How thoroughly he rejects it, flies from it, desires it prevented. 'Let this cup pass from me.' Yet he fails and the crucifiers have their way."[10]

It is difficult to see how such an uninspiring person could be the same one by whom "all things were made." (*John* 1:3). But He is. Jesus Christ is as St. Paul tells us,

> the image of the invisible God, the firstborn of every creature: for in him were all things created in the heaven and on earth, visible and invisible, whether thrones, or dominations, or principalities, or powers: all things were created by him and in him. And he is before all, and by him all things consist. (*Col.* 1:15-17).

One has to ask: Where is Fr. Fox getting this picture of Christ? In his latest book, *The Coming of the Cosmic Christ,* Fox laments Jesus' "cruel and premature death."[11] He says that "no one can ever bring back the time that Jesus lost and will never live out. His was truly an untimely death if ever there was one."[12] Such a statement from a seminary-trained Catholic priest reflects more than ignorance or misunderstanding. It is

---

8. Matthew Fox, *Original Blessing,* p. 307.
9. *Ibid.,* p. 122.
10. Matthew Fox, *Whee! We, wee...,* p. 93.
11. Matthew Fox, *The Coming of the Cosmic Christ* (San Francisco: Harper & Row, 1988), p. 71.
12. *Ibid.,* p. 140.

a denial, a rejection of Christ's mission, a mission which was not cut short, was not untimely, and which was flawlessly fulfilled in accordance with a schedule written in eternity.

Fr. Fox seems not to have heard that Jesus Christ is alive after having spent just three days in the grave; he seems not to understand the very reason Our Lord was born.

Matthew Fox also sees the miracles of the Bible through the perspective of his Creation Spirituality. Our traditional fall/redemption theology accepts miracles as an intervention by the supernatural into the natural order of things. Fox sees a naturalistic explanation in Christ's miracle of the loaves and the fishes: "The real miracle that Jesus wrought was not a quantitative magic trick of turning five loaves and two fishes into thousands. The true miracle was that Jesus got people to let go, to share with one another."[13]

In *A Spirituality Named Compassion,* Fox insists that Our Lord was not good because He was God, but instead was divine because He was good. This denies the infinite connotation of the word "divine" as it applies to Jesus only. Fr. Fox is redefining the word "divine." Specifically, he writes: "Jesus is not so much compassionate because he is divine as he is divine because he is compassionate. And did he...not teach others that they too were...divine because they are compassionate?"[14]

At best, he considers Jesus Christ not as the God who created the universe, but as a sort of drum major out in front of the parade we should all be in. His lip service to Our Lord as the most "creation-centered" human ever to live is mere pandering. One wonders why he wastes good ink on Him.

If Matthew Fox has any historical reference point, it is in the person of the 14th-century German mystic, Meister Eckhart. Eckhart was born around 1260 A.D. and entered the

---

13. Matthew Fox, *Original Blessing,* p. 170.
14. Matthew Fox, *A Spirituality Named Compassion and the Healing of the Global Village, Humpty Dumpty and Us* (Minneapolis, MN: Winston Press, Inc., 1979), p. 34.

Dominican order while a youth. A popular speaker, he had pantheistic ideas that strongly identified God with his creation. Eckhart has been hailed as a forerunner of Theosophists and Pantheists. Hindus regard him as a "kindred spirit."[15] He felt that a God "out there" was unfathomable. Evelyn Underhill, in her book, *The Mystics of the Church*, wrote that Eckhart had

> a tendency to exile God from His creation; and [this] led him to set up a sharp distinction between the Absolute and unconditioned Godhead, "unknown and never to be known," and the God of religious experience. This separation is fundamental to Eckhart's thought...
>
> This leaning to transcendental speculation, land[ed] him at last in a monism which...can hardly be reconciled with Christianity.[16]

Eckhart saw a unity between God and man, and he tended to see Jesus as the first human to realize that unity. Many of his ideas can be taken in more than one sense. The result is that one meaning may be Christian, while the second meaning is solidly heretical. In one of his sermons he said, "If God's being is my being, then God's existence must be my existence and His essence my essence...." In another, he said, "...the Holy Spirit receives His being....from me as from God."[17]

It was his radical ideas, combined with his popularity, that eventually brought him into conflict with the local Church authorities. Near the end of his life, in 1326, he was cited for heresy by a hostile tribunal in his native Germany. Eckhart appealed to the Pope for an unbiased hearing. He agreed to repudiate any teachings which were found to be heretical, but he died before his case was decided.

---

15. James M. Clark, *Meister Eckhart* (London: Thomas Nelson and Sons, 1957), p. vi.
16. Evelyn Underhill, *The Mystics of the Church* (New York: Schocken Books, 1971), p. 134.
17. James M. Clark, *Meister Eckhart*, pp. 187, 141.

In 1329, the year after his death, seventeen of his propositions were condemned as heretical in the bull *In Agro Dominico* of Pope John XII. It was declared that he had been deceived "by the father of lies who often appears as an angel of light" into "sowing thorns and thistles amongst the faithful and even the simple folk."[18] Another eleven statements were considered rash and dangerous, but capable of being interpreted in an orthodox sense. Eckhart's willingness to submit to the Church's authority was reflected in the bull, which stated that he,

> at the end of his life, professed the Catholic faith, revoked and even condemned the...26 articles, which he admitted having preached [as well as] all other matters written or taught by him, either in the schools or in sermons, that might create in the minds of the faithful an heretical or erroneous impression and one hostile to the true faith.[19]

While the German mystic himself was willing to repudiate his teachings, Meister Eckhart's admirers have not been. His unorthodox ideas and speculations have grown in popularity in recent years and have found their most ardent proponent in Fr. Matthew Fox. He gives Eckhart the second highest score on his one-to-five scale of creation-centeredness. More important, Fox has taken Eckhart's condemned teachings and given them his own concrete meanings. Fox quotes Eckhart, declaring, "You may call God love; you may call God goodness; but the best name for God is Compassion."[20] Such a statement may not be heretical, depending on the meaning one gives to it. But in Fr. Fox's dictionary, compassion means that sort of connection with nature exemplified by the practice of witchcraft and other nature religions.

---

18. Raymond B. Blakney, *Meister Eckhart: A Modern Translation* (Harper, 1941), pp. xx-xxiv.
19. James M. Clark, *Meister Eckhart*, p. 258.
20. Matthew Fox, *A Spirituality Named Compassion*, p. 34.

The Craft

What is this twisted meaning Fox gives to the word "compassion"? This "compassion" is (supposedly) the source of every virtue. It is the quality that makes us (and Jesus Christ) divine. The practice of visualization appears as Fox's "extrovert meditation," which he explains as listening to the inner self and uttering "the new images from within outwards. This giving birth to new images is the work of all creative persons."[21]

Compassion is explained in the following excerpt from *A Spirituality Named Compassion*. The word "craft" is a common euphemism for witchcraft. Another is the term "wicca" or "wikke":

> Extrovert meditation, then, gives birth to this new kind of power...a power-with, [which] is properly called compassion. It is a power to imagine with others and to be changed by this imagining. Crafts initiate one into a new kind of power. The German word for power is Kraft. There is no cover-up in this kind of power. "We can't fake craft. It lies in the act...We do not have the craft or craftmanship, if we do not speak to the light that lives within the earthly materials; this means ALL earthly materials, including men themselves."
>
> Compassion is (the realization of the interconnectedness of all things).[22]

The discussion of the "craft" or witchcraft need not be limited to the traditional image of the medieval wart-nosed hag stirring a bubbling cauldron. Rather, it encompasses most of what would commonly be called paganism. Matthew Fox expands the definition in *Original Blessing:*

> Native American spirituality is a creation-centered tradition, as are the other prepatriarchal religions of the world such as African religions, Celtic religion, and the matrifocal and Wikke traditions that scholars and practi-

---

21. *Ibid.*, p. 134.
22. *Ibid.*, pp. 136, 139.

tioners like Starhawk are recovering. The contemporary mystical movement known as "New Age" can also dialogue and create with the creation spiritual tradition.[23]

Miriam Simos (Starhawk) is a practicing witch on the staff of Matthew Fox's Institute for Culture and Creation Spirituality (ICCS). Her specialty is the teaching of ritual. Constance Cumbey calls her "one of the world's most politically active and important witches. She is a high priestess in a major coven and has been [active] politically in both the witches/Neopagan movements as well as the feminist movement. She is a frequent speaker at New-Age convocations and conferences."[24] Starhawk writes: "In the Craft, we do not believe in the Goddess— we connect with her; through the moon, the stars, the ocean, the earth, through trees, animals, through other human beings, through ourselves. She is here. She is within us all."[25]

Witchcraft, which is often called "the old religion," is the worship of (or connection with) "the goddess" or the divine which it finds in nature. Typical of paganism and the Craft are beliefs in female deities, the sacredness of nature, the power of the individual will, and the nonexistence of Original Sin or any division between good or evil. This is the foundation of feminism.

Christianity and Feminism

Feminist spirituality has nothing to do with the issues of fair play and equal pay for equal work. These are rights that Christians can support. Feminism at its root is anti-Catholic, anti-Church and anti-Christ.

What the feminists want covers a wide spectrum. Some want absolute identity between the roles of men and women in the Church. They support abortion on demand, lesbian rights and

23. Matthew Fox, *Original Blessing,* p. 16.
24. Constance Cumbey, *A Planned Deception,* p. 139.
25. Starhawk, *The Spiral Dance: A Rebirth of the Ancient Religion of the Great Goddess* (New York: 1979), p. 77ff.

in general can be found in the liberal wing politically. These are the moderates.

The mainspring groups, however, are not looking for a role in the Church—as we know it—at all. They are devoted to "the goddess" who is found in nature and in themselves; this again is creation-centered spirituality. Their Wikkan rituals tap the "goddess" power. They would drag God from His Heaven and install the mother goddess. While they insist on the goddess, the sexual aspect is secondary to the real appeal—the appeal of having a deity *which they can control.* She empowers them but makes no demands. She takes no offense at sin, nor calls for any redemption in the traditional sense.

The feminists' dominant mode of operation is to create discontent. They foster frustration, resentment and delusions of persecution by the "unjust patriarchal structures" in the Church, while simultaneously extending the promise of the goddess within. To some the appeal to power and pride seems irresistible. The old beliefs lose their grip, and Hell signs up another future tenant. The point at which one crosses over to the other side comes sooner than most imagine. On the other hand, the Church has not been hasty in drawing that line. Consequently, the neo-pagans have a forum for their views. Some of the most public displays occur when feminism's "Catholic" adherents gather. Such events are invariably blasphemous.

March 9-16, 1985 at Mundelein College in Chicago was the time to celebrate "The Goddess and the Wild Woman." The brochure cover sported a woman with one breast exposed, dancing and with flowers springing up beneath her feet. The ancient goddesses Artemis, Athena, Demeter and others stood by. Inside, the brochure spoke of drawing "aside the curtain woven by patriarchal consciousness to reveal within each of us the Goddess and the Wild Woman."[26]

Another gathering of more than 2,000 "Catholic" feminists (as usual, mostly nuns) took place in Washington, D.C. on

---

26. Frank Morris, "Conjuring up Some Strange Spirit," *The Wanderer,* 25 April 1985, p. 4.

October 10-12, 1986. The conference was entitled "Woman in the Church." Just a sample of the fare:

Speaker Sister Madonna Kolbenschlag ripped through the papacy, the Church, Western civilization, the Judaeo-Christian tradition, the Trinity ("a good ole boy, associating with two other divine males") and monotheism. She asked the participants, in the name of "our elder brother, Jesus," to "be a scandal to the patriarchy." Further,

> Someone once asked me, "What can we salvage from the traditional god-myth that is not destructive?" I don't think that salvaging is any concern of ours. Faith is the process of continually replacing the metaphors for god.... Women today must reclaim their reality from the fantasies, especially through the power of a holistic sexuality, and the right to a free and personally responsible expression of it.... [27]

Among the other festivities was a rally in support of Seattle Archbishop Raymond Hunthausen, as well as the inevitable exhibits by pro-abortion and lesbian groups. There was even a group sponsoring a "feminist liturgy" with a "consecration" by the woman attending. Participants sang and recited poetry and chanted "My name is [X] and I claim my power as church." The would-be "priestesses" proclaimed, "We are empowered by a loving goddess. We proclaim the power of our foremothers." They spoke of "our exodus from the patriarchal church...." Then at the "consecration": "We bless this bread of the eucharist of Woman Church." [28]

A reporter asked keynote speaker Sister Joan Chittister if the American Church as an institution was ready to stand in opposition to Rome. "Do you want an answer or a prayer?" she replied. "Oh, God, I hope so!" [29]

27. Donna Steichen, "The Goddess Goes to Washington," *Fidelity,* December, 1986, p. 42.
28. Joseph Sobran, "Catholic Feminists Gather in Washington," *The Wanderer,* 23 October 1986, p. 1.
29. Steichen, *Fidelity,* p. 36.

A feminist philosopher has written of the irreconcilable differences between Christianity and feminism:

> I imagined women functioning as rabbis, priests and ministers...wearing clerical garb and performing clerical duties and suddenly I saw a problem. How could women represent a male god?
>
> God is going to change....We women are going to bring an end to God....we will be the end of Him. We will change the world so much that He won't fit in any more.
>
> Jesus Christ cannot symbolize the liberation of women....Feminists have to leave Christ and Bible behind them.[30]

This feminist spirituality is probably the most blatant form of heresy in the Church today. One wonders how far the leaders of the movement can go without waking up those who, as yet, follow unwittingly. It is not as if the feminists are going around on tiptoe. "Catholic" feminist theologian Rosemary Ruether writes about her own experience:

> I knew that Ba'al was a real god, the revelation of the mystery of life, the expressions of the depths of being which had broken through into the lives of the people and gave them a key to the mystery of death and rebirth....As for the defects of Ba'al, were they more spectacular than the defects of the biblical God or Messiah, or perhaps less so?
>
> I could hardly tell her [a nun] that my devotion to Mary was somewhat less than my devotion to some far more powerful females that I knew: Isis, Athena, and Artemis![31]

James Hitchcock has pointed out that Rosemary Ruether held these opinions as an undergraduate, "and thus held them

---

30. Naomi R. Goldenberg, *Changing Of The Gods: Feminism and the End of Traditional Religions* (Boston: Beacon Press, 1979), pp. 3, 22.

31. Gregory Baum, ed., *Journeys: The Impact of Personal Experience on Religious Thought* (New York: Paulist Press, 1975), pp. 43-45.

throughout the period when she had a public identity as an orthodox Catholic theologian."[32]

In an April, 1985 interview, Ruether was asked why she even bothered to stay within the Church when so many others with her beliefs had left. Her answer might have come from any one of thousands of modernist Catholics in the Church today: "As a feminist, I can come up with only one reason to stay in the Catholic Church: to try to change it."[33]

The Infection Spreads

U.S. Catholics are not the only ones being exposed to this "tradition." Our brethren to the North are not free of the "WomanChurch" phenomenon. The Canadian Bishops have allowed the use of a "Study Kit" on women's issues. The bibliography of this material recommends the works of radical feminist theologians. One of twelve sessions "contains a liturgy drawn from Wiccan (witchcraft) sources." One report on the kit maintained that women claimed the experience had given them a "greater sense of dignity."[34] (Apparently the discovery of your goddess-hood does that for you!)

How far can the return to paganism go? In many places it has gone far. A *National Catholic Reporter* headline reads, "Archbishop summoned for 'witchcraft.'"[35] In Germany, there is an officially registered school for witchcraft. A pharmaceutical company produces tincture of cannabis and other drugs used to enhance pagan rituals.[36] We should take warning from the situation in Brazil, where voodoo cults thrive.

---

32. James Hitchcock, *Catholicism and Modernity: Confrontation or Capitulation?* (New York: Seabury Press, 1979), p. 186.
33. "The Editors Interview Rosemary Radford Ruether," *U.S. Catholic,* April 1985, p. 19.
34. "Canadian Bishops' 'Study Kit,'" *The Wanderer* (Ottawa: Rueters News Service), 23 October 1986, p. 1.
35. Peter Hebblethwaite, "Archbishop Summoned for 'Witchcraft,'" *National Catholic Reporter,* 10 September 1982, p. 26.
36. "German Ghouls" ("Insight" section), *America,* 17 Nov. 1984, p. 315.

On most nights, thousands of followers of the old African religion offer animal sacrifices and while in trances worship spirits which have been merged (in *their* minds) with the worshippers' favorite Catholic saints. Each cultist is assigned particular spirits who symbolize Christ, the Virgin Mary and other saints, but are actually demons carried over from the old religion.

The Catholic Church in Brazil is the largest of any country in the world. Ninety percent of Brazil's 131 million people are officially Catholic, and it is estimated that this mixture of African ritualism and Catholicism is practiced by nearly half of all Brazilian Catholics. The clergy shrug at the problem, admitting that if Rome ordered the pagan practices stopped, no one would listen. One priest said that official Church policy opposes the cults, "but if we had a hard, inflexible attitude, we would lose them all."

In the Catholic Church in the United States, we too can be seen to have slipped far when we come to realize that witchcraft, or pre-Christian paganism, is merely another facet of the New-Age Movement. Even Fr. Matthew Fox admits that his Western-oriented Creation Spirituality is part of the same picture. His Institute for Culture and Creation Spirituality (ICCS) has "become a focus for dialogue with native and Eastern spiritual traditions, the human potential movement, the new physics and the Green Movement."

He says, "Christians and others should not be afraid of terms like 'New Age.' The 'new' can in fact prove to be quite old. For example, a 'new' theology of original blessing is in fact far more ancient than the familiar theology of original sin."

Finally, as to make certain that no one misses all the connections, the last page of Fox's five-point Creation-Centered honor roll reads like a "Who's Who in the New Age Movement":

- Teilhard de Chardin
- Carl Jung, psychologist/occultist

- Buckminster Fuller, author of *Spaceship Earth*
- Fritjof Capra, author of *The Tao of Physics*
- Starhawk, author of *Dreaming the Dark*
- Marilyn Ferguson, author of *The Aquarian Conspiracy*
- David Spangler, author of *Revelation: Birth of a New Age*

Of course, many of these authors return the favor and often recommend the others for New Age reading. David Spangler's Lorien Press distributes exclusively New Age titles, some of which were actually dictated by demons. Lorien offers Fox's *Original Blessing,* calling it "a seminal work which Lorien Press is proud to offer."

It is difficult to say how much more popular the New Age Movement will become in future years. What is certain is that Christianity is the prime force holding it back. Catholics are the big prize. Unfortunately, the Church, which should be the "salt of the Earth," finds itself here in need of "savor." (*Matt.* 5:13). If individual Catholics do not act as that salt and stand clearly across the path of this giant, then Fr. Matthew Fox's hope may yet come true:

> Beginning with artists in the nineteenth century and extending today to scientists, feminists, New Age mystics, and social prophets, a veritable explosion of creation-centered spiritual energy is and has been occurring. If entire religious bodies such as Christianity could enter into this expanding spiritual energy field, there is no predicting what powers of passion and compassion might become unleashed.

Fr. Fox is an insightful man. He sees a need within the Church and moves to fill the vacuum. He points out that we have lost some of the mystery and darkness of the liturgy. The Latin, the smell of many candles and incense, and the somber tones of the Gregorian chant are gone—and gone with these, some sense of holiness and awe.

Having noted the need for "darkness" and ritual, Fr. Fox has a program. He guides us to Native American sweat lodges, to ceremonial dances with drums and fire, and to the witch's Moon Ritual.[37]

While Fr. Matthew Fox's work continues to grow in popularity in America, his teachings have not gone unnoticed in Rome. After a four-year-long investigation of his works, Fox's own Dominican Order silenced him for one year. Fox announced that the Order had acted "under pressure from the Vatican Congregation of the Doctrine of the Faith, formerly known as the Holy Office of the Inquisition." In Fox's statement to the press on October 20, 1988, he said that it was "an honor to be silenced by the present regime in the Vatican. . . .The Vatican has grown deaf—deaf to the cries of Mother Earth, deaf to the cries of women, of native peoples and persons of color, of artists. . . ." He spoke of the "need for a spirituality which can heal Mother Earth and usher in an era of a Global Renaissance. . . .I am proud to be a part of that movement."

Fr. Fox's organization, the Friends of Creation Spirituality (FCS), announced that Fr. Fox would begin a sabbatical on December 15, 1988 and that he anticipated returning to the Institute for Creation-Centered Spirituality in the fall of 1989. FCS also initiated a letter-writing campaign to support Fox and the spread of Creation Spirituality. Like his proud Modernist forebears, it appears that Fr. Matthew Fox will carry on the tradition of minimal outward submission coupled with contemptuous defiance.

---

37. Matthew Fox, *Cosmic Christ,* pp. 220-21.

7.

Close to Home

If your parish has not been the scene of New Age stirrings and teachings, it is a real blessing. Some parish priests are completely sold on the New Age Movement. Others are obviously influenced by it, perhaps without knowing it. But even if the pastor is faithful, even if he is rock solid, in a large parish he may be undermined by others to whom he must turn for assistance. If that were not enough, he may shepherd a fine parish and still see his flock infected. Unless the bishop is equally vigilant, there is no guarantee of safety in sending parishioners into diocesan programs.

Sometimes parishioners are only sporadically subjected to New Age references. Maybe Father just read something that he liked and threw it into the homily this week. Last Advent I heard an assistant pastor say, "This is the time of year we remember when a man became God." Now that did not sound quite right.

On Trinity Sunday we were treated to a sermon on how we need to see God "not just as Father-Son-Spirit, but as Mother-Daughter-Spirit," because that is just as legitimate a viewpoint as the male God perspective. A week later we were given Part Two on "seeing God as mother." There is certainly nothing wrong with saying that God has what have traditionally been thought of as feminine qualities, such as nurturing.

How else to explain Jesus's lament over Jerusalem: "How often would I have gathered together thy children, as the hen doth gather her chickens under her wings, and thou wouldest not?" (*Matt.* 23:37). But then, God has chosen to reveal Himself as Father. It is as if He were telling us that while He is not a man, He can reveal Himself to us best as "Father."

The feminists will argue that God/the Goddess revealed herself/himself as a male (Father and Son) because that was necessary in the culture of Biblical times. That much said, they then prove exactly the opposite in their tirade against the patriarchal systems of the Judeo-Christian tradition. They claim that before God appeared to Abraham, religion was matriarchal. The feminists then correctly point out that even throughout the history of the Old Testament, the Israelites' neighbors worshipped both male and female gods. Logically then, if the idea of a female deity was common, why should God have had any practical need to conform to patriarchal customs?

The best explanation is the simplest. He revealed Himself in exactly the way in which He desired to be known. It is our duty as His creatures to accept it.

Catholics of Orange, California were recently treated to a Buddhist healing service at the Spirituality Center for the Sisters of St. Joseph of Orange. Five Tibetan monks chanted mantras and rang bells. Wearing headdresses topped with skulls, the monks danced, banged a drum and tooted a horn. At intermission, Buddhist and New Age materials were offered for sale.

"As a Christian, I'm afraid to read this," said one Catholic woman.

"With all bad things, there's some good," replied the reassuring Sister as she collected the cash.

A brief talk on Buddhism followed, and then the pagan

ritual concluded with a dance, for which the monks put on a horse costume.[1]

For two weeks straight the Sunday bulletin trumpeted the upcoming speaking engagement of Rosemary Ruether at the University of Missouri campus Newman Center on April 29, 1988. The rainbow backdrop to the altar was appropriate for the occasion, as this professor of theology railed against the unjust patriarchal structures of the Church. Describing her own spirituality as a "creation-based spirituality" (remember Matthew Fox?), she explained her resistance to "spiritualities which make other worldly splits." This is pantheism. It rejects the distinction between nature and spirit which Scripture clearly reveals and the Church teaches.

Speaking of redemption and Jesus Christ (who "got himself strung up"), she said, "Nobody can save the world by himself. The only way you can save the whole world is by all of us together." A few of Ruether's listeners shifted uneasily in their seats, but most were in accord. Could she—even as she stood at the altar in front of the crucified Christ—could she have forgotten that "By a man came death, and by a man the resurrection of the dead. And as in Adam all die, so also in Christ all shall be made alive." (*1 Cor.* 15:21-22).[2] Naturally, we must co-operate in this salvation, but the individual will stand or fall on his own faith and corresponding works. Whether together or separately, we humans will never save the world.

This is a great lie of the New Age Movement and shows a striking similarity to a supposedly non-religious belief—that

---

1. *The Wanderer,* 23 November 1989, p. 8.
2. Actually, the feminists studiously avoid this verse, because it undermines their favorite myth: that the Church persecutes women because it considers *them* responsible for Original Sin. Without this and other paranoid accusations they would be much less effective in getting their listeners lathered up for a fight (in fact, the formation of a Woman-Church group was the objective of this particular get-together).

of secular humanism. The *Humanist Manifesto II* declares: "Humans are responsible for what we are or will become. No deity will save us; we must save ourselves." The apparent difference between the "mystical" New Age view and the agnostic Secular Humanist view is no real difference at all. Both viewpoints are in perfect agreement in believing that nature is everything and we don't need God. Each exalts both human potential and scientific progress. Each makes man a god, answerable only to himself. One is hard-pressed to draw dividing lines that differentiate New Age from Secular Humanism other than by degree.

Sometimes "Catholic" New Agers will form parachurch organizations open to all faiths, and thus not specifically Catholic, but with a strong Catholic membership, Catholic outreach and support in the Catholic community. In Kansas City, Missouri, WomanSource is such an organization. WomanSource founder and former president Carol Meyer is an ex-nun who "saw a need for more support in the community for the empowerment of women." She is also the former associate director of the editorial department of Credence Cassettes, a division of the National Catholic Reporter publishing company and a leading "Catholic" purveyor of New Age tapes. She and eleven other women, including another nun (a Sister of Charity), started the group in October, 1986. Funded by dues, donations and grants, they received their first grant, $1000, from the Sisters of Loretto.

WomanSource operates a "drop-in center" which includes a meditation room. A friend who has visited the center described a "stark room with a round rug on the floor. On the rug was a small clay pot for a candle. Also on the rug was a statue of a woman, and behind the statue, leaning against the wall, was a very large framed picture of Stonehenge." My friend wondered what god they prayed to in that room. Her guide said, "I am a Catholic, but anyone can pray to whoever they feel like or want to."

The April/May, 1988 issue of the WomanSource newsletter

promoted a "self-awareness group" which was scheduled to meet for six consecutive Saturdays and would—among other things—explore "matriarchal societies' histories and *how to use the goddess' energy for personal empowerment.*" Even if such paganism received no actual support from the Church, it would still be worth warning Catholic women about what they are getting into. But the Kansas City diocese does not merely acquiesce in the matter; it is actually a warm home for WomanSource. Consider how likely local Catholics are to take warning when even the official diocesan paper has run a positive article on WomanSource and has carried WomanSource events in the weekly calendar. The same holds when local Catholic churches open their facilities to the group.

On February 26, 1988 WomanSource offered a retreat at the Franciscan Prayer Center in Independence, Missouri. Called "The Healing Art of Meditation," the experience was to include such topics as "Tibetan Buddhism, Visualization, Centering, Chakra Balancing, Sufi Blessing, *Tai-Chi* and Clay Meditation."

Another group, Woman Alive, presented a program called WomanSpirit Rising (funny how these New Age feminists always run the word "woman" and something else together). This New Age event was held at the Maria Center of the School Sisters of Notre Dame in St. Louis, Missouri, over Halloween weekend, 1987. Jolene Unnerstall, coordinator for Woman Alive and ex-Sister of Notre Dame, was joined by fellow Aquarians in presenting workshops involving pure pagan occultism. A few of their "Out on a Limb" style topics:

THE GODDESS WITHIN
Recognition of the archetypal patterns of ancient Goddesses inspires us to appreciate the power and presence of divine qualities within ourselves and to enjoy recognizing the unique beauty of the goddesses in our friends and family.

PAST LIVES and PRESENT WISDOM

Jolene has served as a reader of Akashic records as well as led hundreds of seekers to explore their own past-life memories. We will explore the purpose and value of uncovering past life wisdom and applying it to today's experience.

CHAKRAS: Spiritual Energy Centers

The "chakra" system of understanding our spiritual energy is a tool for wholesomeness. We will experience a meditation for chakra balancing. . . .

CHANNELING YOUR HIGH SELF

Explore the techniques and processes of channeling and how to use channeled information to enhance spiritual understanding. Group channeling will be the highlight of the session. Participants can plan to get some questions of a spiritual nature answered through the channeling process.

CYRSTALS for MEDITATION

Crystals can be used as a tool for amplifying consciousness and as such can be an aid to focusing in meditation and healing. Presents how to select and use crystals wisely.

How can it be that Catholics would get involved with such unmixed spiritual venom? Largely because they assume that no Catholic institution would permit its facilities to be used for such things as the calling up of demons for the purpose of giving advice. Maybe one should not assume anything anymore.

One of the most remarkable New Age successes has to be the breeziness with which New Age meditation is recommended—even in the church—for any Catholic who is interested. I read this notice in our parish bulletin and decided to check it out for myself:

CENTERING PRAYER: Fr. Bob will make a presentation on "Centering Prayer," a method of meditation, on

Monday, March 2, at 7:45 p.m. in Classroom 2 in the parish hall. All are invited.

Our assistant pastor began speaking to our group, which was made up of eight or ten women plus myself. He introduced the topic, explaining that in 1976, Pope Paul VI asked a leader of the Cistercian Order to share his order's prayer methods with other religious communities. More than a decade later, the Pope's request now serves as the reason that our self-appointed little group was about to be taught Hindu meditation. Father began:

"The purpose of the technique is to move our minds to a different state of consciousness. The idea is that the experience should sustain us during the time we are not meditating. We go to a deeper level, searching for God or Jesus, whom we believe to be there. This is accomplished through the use of the *Love Word* [mantra], which is repeated just often enough to keep you centered. Some people feel it helps to tie the Love Word into their breathing. You'll notice how it slows as you go deeper."

"At that level," he concluded, "you feel God. Faith is no longer necessary."

At this point, we moved into the church building to have a go at it ourselves. We sat in the dark pews for 25 minutes. I spent the first ten minutes emptying my brain in hopes that God would start talking or moving or whatever.

"How would I know it was Him?" I had wondered. . . .

"This is ridiculous!" I thought, as I abandoned the effort and instead used the remaining time to initiate a more conventional and effective prayer. Finally, Father spoke, bringing us back to our normal waking level of consciousness and dismissing us with his hope that meditation would become a frequent and profitable experience. It seemed a frivolous ending for what might for some turn out to be very deep water.

I expressed my concern to one friend, who although favorably disposed to such meditation from his seminary experience, was disturbed at the dangers of its indiscriminate spread and these unguided pilgrimages into the unknown. Another priest friend listened to my concerns about New Age meditation and the Church and just shrugged. "We have much to learn from the Hindus," he told me.

The New Age on Tape

What can a Catholic New Ager do to accelerate his downward slide if he has no New-Age center in his town and if his pastor will not let the poison in the church door? He can find plenty of New-Age books and tapes, and he will not have to step outside "Catholic" sources to do it. Such Catholic suppliers as Credence Cassettes (a service of the National Catholic Reporter Publishing Co.) and Paulist Press promote the rubbish. Even Orbis Books (Maryknoll Fathers) has given the New Age some catalog space—while still carrying the full line of their trademark "liberation theology" titles. A few of the topics/authors available from Credence Cassettes:

- Mantra Chanting; the "Groaning Prayer Cassette."
- A Jesuit theologian who has traveled in Asia and studied Eastern prayer teaches Hatha Yoga.
- Guided Meditations/Imagery.
- Lots of New Age (healing) music.
- The seven petitions of the LORD'S Prayer are correlated with the seven occult energy centers from the East *(chakras)*. The speaker explains how these petitions and chakras describe various postures. With New Age music accompaniment.
- Dream Interpretation and the occultist/psychologist C.G. Jung.
- Ed Hays, Bede Griffiths, Thomas Merton.
- Ira Progoff journaling; The Spirituality of Teilhard de Chardin.
- WOMANCHURCH/Rosemary Ruether.

How ironic that this same catalog had a cassette entitled "Traditional Catholic Hymns" marked down to half price.

Silva Mind Control

It would be difficult to find a system of practice more destructive of Christian faith than the Silva Mind Control Method. More difficult yet is it to imagine it being promoted and taught in a Catholic church. The system features both the meditative state of Eastern religion and the pagan visualization techniques which give the method its power. In the Silva Method, the student first learns to achieve an altered state of consciousness ("counting down to your level"). Through a series of meditations he learns relaxation and problem solving.

The student begins to utilize visualization by creating a "Mental Screen" within the imagination. He projects onto the screen whatever image he wishes to concentrate upon. The meditations purport to ease pain, speed learning and break bad habits. These, though, are just the baby steps of this method.

On the third day of training, students learn to project themselves, through their imaginations, into buildings, walls, metal objects and even inside the body of a pet (in preparation for projections into human bodies). Finally, the student is ready to construct his laboratory. In deep meditation, the mind-control student creates a refuge of his choosing—a cozy library, a submarine, a cave or whatever he likes. It is furnished with desk and chair, filing cabinets, clock and calendar. Additionally, the student adds various tools: healing salves, chemicals, a stereo playing soothing music.

In the laboratory, the meditating student summons two "counselors," male and female. These "counselors" are to be consulted in full confidence. Their guidance supposedly confers great power (for good only, of course). Upon their appearance in the laboratory, these counselors may or may not turn out to be the persons the student had hoped for. Who are these "counselors" Mr. Silva provides? In *The Silva Mind Control Method,* he answers:

> We are not sure—perhaps some figment of our archetypal imagination, perhaps an embodiment of the inner voice, perhaps something more. What we do know is that, once we meet our counselors and learn to work with them, the association is respectful and priceless.[3]

In her book, *The Beautiful Side of Evil,* Johanna Michaelsen tells of her experience with the Silva Method. She chose Jesus and Sarah Bernhardt (Johanna was interested in acting) as her counselors. At the Mind Control class, she went to her level and entered her laboratory where her counselors, Jesus and Sarah, revealed themselves to her. She fell at Jesus' feet.

Before dismissing the class, the instructor admonished the students not to try to call up their counselors that evening at home. That night, ignoring the warning, she counted down to her level, and as she sat in the blue velvet armchair in her laboratory facing the door:

> "Oh Lord," I prayed, "please, reveal the counselors I'm truly meant to have." The chamber door began lowering—the same radiance shining from behind it—but something was wrong...The hair was wild and matted, the forehead was covered with coarse fur and the eyes were slanted, gleaming and wild...Fresh blood smeared the muzzle and oozed down long white fangs...Yet the rest of the figure was the same as before, covered in a long linen robe and gleaming.[4]

The next day at mind-control class—discounting the experience the night before—Johanna learned to accept the

---

3. José Silva, Phillip Miele, *The Silva Mind Control Method* (New York: Simon and Schuster, 1977), p. 87.

4. Johanna Michaelsen, *The Beautiful Side of Evil* (Eugene, Oregon: Harvest House, 1982), p. 75.

werewolf faces of Jesus and Sarah. That day she learned to psychically diagnose the illnesses of people far away whom she had never met.

Later, she became the assistant to a psychic surgeon whose body was possessed by a spirit being who performed surgery with unsterilized knives and scissors and without anesthetic.[5] Her story shows that evil can appear as beautiful as anyone can imagine.

As with other meditation systems, Silva Mind Control is supposed to be absolutely harmless. José Silva claims that it is impossible to do evil while at your meditative level.[6] On the other hand, the spirit being who controlled the psychic surgeon informed Johanna that "a person who wishes another one evil strongly enough can cause dark beings to focus upon him."[7] It has to make one wonder why openly occult sources seem willing to admit to the dangers of esoteric meditation but the supposed "self-improvement" types and "Christian" supporters of the techniques fall all over themselves in denying the dangers.

What has this to do with the Roman Catholics? We are signing up at $325 apiece (the cost of the Silva course) to learn to control these powers. I am reminded of St. Peter's reaction to Simon the magician, who was so impressed with the Apostles' power that he attempted to buy it. Peter replied, "Keep thy money to thyself, to perish with thee, because thou hast thought that the gift of God may be purchased with money." (*Acts* 8:20).

Most recently I ran into literature from a group in Indianapolis called "The Hermitage." While "The Hermitage" calls itself an ecumenical organization, its founding director is a Catholic priest who teaches the Silva Method as well as other meditation courses. The Hermitage offers courses in

5. *Ibid.,* pp. 77, 85.
6. José Silva, *Silva Mind Control,* p. 35.
7. Michaelsen, *The Beautiful Side of Evil,* p. 133.

The Silva Method of Mind Development, Silva Method for Children (done with puppets), Christian Astrology & Buddhist meditation. Its newsletter attracts advertisers offering occult books and Yoga therapy, numerology services, shamanism, private healings and the like.

While this outfit is not an overtly "Catholic" enterprise, Catholic organizations seem to be open to it. I called a Catholic parish in Omaha that was offering the Hermitage's Silva Method that same week. The secretary verified the ongoing (four-day) course. I asked whether some people objected to having this course in the church. "Oh no," she told me, "Father [the pastor] has had these here in prior years."

I spoke with the Omaha coordinator for the Hermitage (also a Catholic). She said the best thing about the course was the realization of being "at one with others and with the universe." I asked, "Do you see any similarity between Silva meditation and what is now called Centering Prayer?"

"It's all *exactly* the same thing!" she insisted. "All of these things [meditation techniques] are the same thing." She invited me to the course on "Successful Living"—achieving success through meditation—which was scheduled for the coming weekend. I passed up the opportunity, figuring that if I needed that sort of thing I could find it a lot closer to home. For it is not in Omaha alone that someone seems to be asleep at the wheel. I noticed from their schedule that the next stop on the Hermitage's Silva Method road show was to be a convent in Cleveland.

8.

Fight It?. . .or Forget It?

I hope someone would criticize a book like this. I hope they would ask why it should even be written. Why drag up all this ugly material and cite the involvement of members of our own Church? My answer would be to agree. After all, we have the Church to show us the truth. We have the Bible, God's Word, to shine its light through the mess.

Ideally, our church leaders will be faithful, but some are not. Two great strengths of the Catholic Church—our hierarchy and institutions—are no strengths unless the shepherds are faithful at every level. Many Catholics, regrettably, have allowed their trust in the hierarchy to deaden their capacity to think for themselves.

When the sermon leaves you scratching your head, do not immediately question your Catholic education or your intelligence. The most common reaction of people exposed to New Age ideas from the pulpit is to assume that there must be something faulty in themselves whenever ideas in sermons strike a strange-sounding chord. But one need not be a theologian to realize that the homily is rotten when the subject is the "Mother Goddess."

It is the greatest irony that the very Catholics who seek to serve God and hunger most for Him are the most endangered. Having no reason to mistrust their seminary professor, local pastor or diocesan officials, they hand their spiritual development over to those who would destroy them. They get involved in C.C.D. programs or become Communion ministers or lectors. Typically, and reasonably, they are expected to take a series of courses to prepare them for these responsibilities. They go on retreats or other weekend programs for spiritual growth. Too often, though, they are taught to devalue the Scriptures, to discount the miracles and divinity of Christ, and to bare their minds to the spiritual dynamite of Eastern meditation. If they refuse to swallow the lies of the "new spirituality," they can look forward to being ridiculed by eloquent, educated teachers.

Ideally, Catholics will study for themselves the Bible and good Catholic books, imitating the Bereans of the New Testament who "received the word with all eagerness, daily searching the scriptures, whether these things were so." (*Acts* 17:11). But we have not. Sadly, some of our most effective barriers to error have come down.

It should be clear that many unwary and innocent Catholics are being pulled in. Catholic clergy and laity are joining the New Age at least as eagerly as the rest of the world. A Jesuit professor of philosophy confesses to being a believer in astrology. One Catholic astrologer who has had many priests come to her for advice has said: "Now a lot of Catholics in my congregation come to me either as students or clients. The clergy have never given me a problem; only Catholics who consider it superstitious and fundamentalists who interpret the Bible very literally and often incorrectly."[1]

A Catholic theologian has written a book attempting to reconcile Christian belief with psychic phenomena. He calls Jesus a "human being...blessed and gifted with incredible paranormal and psychokinetic powers."[2]

---

1. Brian Baker, "Can Catholics Believe in Astrology? Yes and no," *Our Sunday Visitor,* 26 January 1986, p. 8.
2. John J. Heaney, *The Sacred and the Psychic: Parapsychology & Christian Theology* (New York: Paulist Press, 1984), p. 43.

On another front, Catholic publishers have been eager to produce New Age books and other materials. Whether they know what they do, or are simply following the crowd, who can say? But what is not doubtful is the unmistakable fact of the shift. I have watched the cassette catalog published by the *National Catholic Reporter* (see Chapter Seven) grow more and more New Age with each issue. Its offerings now include much material formerly found only in occult book stores.

Also, we must remain watchful outside the church doors as well. Not everyone is making an entrance into the New Age Movement through spiritual pathways. Many enter in through various other modes of transformation. True, the New Age Movement is firstly a spiritual movement, but additionally, it is a total movement encompassing all aspects of life, including politics and economics. In the business community, the New Age concept of visualization is the basis of success tapes and seminars. In the schools, it surfaces as global education, emphasizing social values and "planetary consciousness" while downplaying reading, math and national independence.

Darkness Ahead?

Often the "new ideas" are appealing. Not all New Age solutions are bad—at least not at first glance. Still other New Age goals are quite hopeless, but people, nonetheless, are willing to grasp for them in desperation.

Some time ago, a television movie called *The Day After* aired. Its portrayal of the aftermath of nuclear war was particularly dismaying and ominous. The next day, I was discussing the program with a friend who was more than a little discouraged by it. He volunteered his solution to the problem of nuclear war:

"I've figured out that there is only one way out of this."

I smiled and said, "Really?" I thought a joke was coming.

"Well, sure," he said, "the only permanent solution is to

have a single world government!" He was brightening now as the thought solidified in his mind, obviously delighted with himself.

"It will never work," I told him.

"Why not?" he asked as his solution developed a crack.

"You'd have to kill too many people," I continued: "Me for one; I'd never go along and I'm sure plenty of others would not either."

He glared at me and for a moment I sensed his anger, even a flash of hatred. It made me strangely uncomfortable. I was not surprised that normally level-headed people would seize upon radical ideas. What was surprising was the grip that those ideas have on them and the disdain that falls on others not similarly transformed. One wonders what the New Agers would do with Christians if they ever obtained political power. Their writings speak of "cleansings" and of removing us from the physical plane. They speak of reducing the population by a billion or two, or three, and of a new natural selection which involves destruction to clear the way for evolutionary progress.

"The Wild Truth"

Books promoting the New Age Movement often display a special pride in enumerating the dozens of entrance-ways into the Movement. In *The Aquarian Conspiracy,* Marilyn Ferguson wrote of "trigger" experiences that focus awareness on awareness. Among the triggers are biofeedback, music meditation, hypnosis, self-hypnosis, seminars like *est* or Silva Mind Control, primal therapy, gestalt therapy, and the martial arts. She also reported the disciplines below as being instrumental in personal change:

- Zen Buddhism
- Yoga
- "Christian" mysticism
- Journals and dream journals

- Psychosynthesis
- Jungian therapy
- Transcendental Meditation
- Tibetan Buddhism
- Sufism
- Transactional analysis[3]

It would seem that the ways into the New Age are as wide and varied as the individuals who enter it. That way is easy and contrasts sharply with the way that Our Lord pointed out:

> Enter ye in at the narrow gate: for wide is the gate, and broad is the way that leadeth to destruction, and many there are who go in thereat. How narrow is the gate, and strait is the way that leadeth to life: And few there are that find it! (*Matt.* 7:13,14).

G.K. Chesterton wrote about the need for orthodoxy. To him the narrow way was not restrictive, but glorious:

> Last and most important, it is exactly this which explains what is so inexplicable to all the modern critics of the history of Christianity. I mean the monstrous wars about small points of theology, the earthquakes of emotion about a gesture or a word. It was only a matter of an inch; but an inch is everything when you are balancing.
>
> Doctrines had to be defined within strict limits, even in order that man might enjoy general human liberties. The Church had to be careful, only if the world might be careless.
>
> This is the thrilling romance of Orthodoxy. People have fallen into the foolish habit of speaking of orthodoxy as something heavy, humdrum and safe. There never was anything so perilous or so exciting as orthodoxy. It was sanity: and to be sane is more dramatic than to be mad. It was the equilibrium of a man behind madly rushing horses.

---

3. Marilyn Ferguson, *The Aquarian Conspiracy,* pp. 85-87.

It is easy to be a madman: It is easy to be a heretic. It is always easy to let the age have its head; the difficult thing is to keep one's own. It is always easy to be a modernist; as it is easy to be a snob. To have fallen into any of those open traps of error and exaggeration which fashion after fashion and sect after sect set along the historic path of Christendom—that would indeed have been simple. It is always simple to fall; there are an infinity of angles at which one falls, only one at which one stands. To have fallen into any one of the fads from Gnosticism to Christian Science would indeed have been obvious and tame. But to have avoided them all has been one whirling adventure, and in my vision the heavenly chariot flies thundering through the ages; the dull heresies sprawling and prostrate, the wild truth reeling but erect.[4]

The Final Confrontation?

In a 1976 visit to the United States, Pope John Paul II (then Karol Cardinal Wojtyla) spoke prophetically of a final crisis coming upon the Church:

> We are now standing in the face of the greatest historical confrontation humanity has gone through. I do not think that wide circles of the American society or wide circles of the Christian community realize this fully. We are now facing the final confrontation between the Church and the anti-Church, of the Gospel versus the anti-Gospel. This confrontation lies within the plans of divine Providence; it is a trial which the whole Church...must take up.[5]

The "confrontation" is assuming an increasingly solid shape, but we still do not have a complete picture.

---

4. G.K. Chesterton, *Orthodoxy* (Garden City, New York: Image Books, 1959), pp. 100-101.
5. "Notable and Quotable," *Wall Street Journal,* 9 November 1978, originally quoted in the *New York City News.*

What we must not do when looking at the New Age Movement is to see just so many separate heresies. The term "networking" was first embraced by New Agers, but has now come into general usage. A useful concept, networking is a method of linking people together in the manner of a fish net. The non-hierarchical structure of the network, with its "knots" or nodes, makes it appear headless and less potent than it really is. But as the fish knows that gets caught in the net, it works very well. The manifestations of the New Age Movement that we see in the Church are truly the tentacles of the same adversary, just as St. Pius X cautioned: "The Modernists. . .present their doctrines without order and systematic arrangement into one whole, scattered and disjointed one from another, so as to appear to be in doubt and uncertainty, while they are in reality firm and steadfast. . . ."[6]

It might even be called a conspiracy, though not in the conventional sense. Most New Agers themselves do not have *the plan* in front of them as they work. Instead, the collusion is one of mutual goals, shared values, and a common spiritual orientation. The reader should not misunderstand. There *is* a real conspiracy, and it is orchestrated from a single source: the Devil in Hell, who wants to take souls there. The fight is about nothing else. It is about standing firm and faithful to God. It is about taking the trouble to question new ideas (however popular) to see if they square with the truth.

We must question seemingly supernatural events. The forces of evil are quite capable of producing signs and wonders. Why are people so eager to chase after such things? We are Christians. We believe in miracles, but we know that Satan is able to counterfeit them also. With this in mind, remember, it is the message that counts. We have been warned:

> Dearly beloved, believe not every spirit, but try the spirits if they be of God: because many false prophets are gone out into this world. By this is the spirit of God

---

6. Pius X, *Pascendi,* p. 6.

> known. Every spirit which confesseth that Jesus Christ
> is come in the flesh, is of God: and every spirit that
> dissolveth Jesus, is not of God: and this is Antichrist
> .... (*1 John* 4:1-3).

"Every spirit that dissolveth Jesus" refers to the separation of Jesus from the "office" of the Christ. This is precisely what the New Agers and the world religion advocates have done. Apparent miracles and religious feelings notwithstanding, if the *message* is un-Christian and un-Catholic, then *it is not of God*. St. Paul could not have been more emphatic when he said:

> But though we, or an angel from heaven, preach a
> gospel to you besides that which we have preached to
> you, let him be anathema. As we said before, so now
> I say again: If any one preach to you a gospel, besides
> that which you have received, let him be anathema.
> (*Gal.* 1:8-9).

Our vigilance should be commensurate with the fury and hatred of our enemy. Surely, the New Age Movement is the hottest trick in his bag.

This book might have been much longer, except that it has not been my purpose to fill in all the blanks, exposing the complete scope of the "conspiracy." It is not for everyone to make a long study of it, but rather to be aware, and to be ready to resist when necessary. Do not think for a moment that lay people are incapable of fighting back.

Once, as a CCD teacher, I was required to attend certain ongoing courses sponsored by the diocese in order to remain a certified teacher. Having been exposed to Matthew Fox's ideas and "encounter-group"-type exercises in earlier classes, I hoped the upcoming class on the Scriptures would be a welcome change. Held on two consecutive Saturdays, the course turned out to be simply an eight-hour attack on the Bible. The first Saturday, the instructor tore apart the Old Testament, stripping it of all historic and prophetic value. A week later, he taught us that the miracles recorded in the New Testament never really happened! He allowed only the Resurrection. (I suppose he was not ready to take that one on!)

In light of the trash we had already been subjected to, I decided I had had enough, and raised my hand. He stopped and I said: "I have always been taught that the Gospel stories are true and that they support the truth of Christianity. Now it is a very nice spring day out, and if all of this is just a fairy story, then we are wasting our time. We ought to go home and do more important things."

I sat back down, feeling more than half like an idiot. The teacher stared for a moment, somehow torn between anger and pity for this ignorant wretch. Just as he was about to open his mouth to crush me, someone else spoke up: "He's right. I believe the same thing."

"Yeah, me too," said another, and another, until all 25 of us had come down in perfect opposition to his propaganda. Did he argue with us? No; he sensed he was beaten and worked quickly to fall into line, backpeddling faster than a politician. I almost think he liked it.

The point is that we lay people are not powerless. In many cases we have more freedom to act than do the clergy. If a faithful priest or nun raises a complaint, he or she may be told to "stay out of it." Imagine how difficult it would be for them to resist such orders to keep their mouths closed and their heads down. They need our support and prayers. The laity, on the other hand, are less easily restrained. Still, our opposition may be costly.

That was the lesson learned by the parishioners at St. Boniface in Stewart, Minnesota. Operating without a resident pastor, the church was assigned a nun as "parish minister." Unfortunately, she was a Matthew Fox devotée who replaced orthodox teachings with worship of self and nature.

Her Saturday "eucharists" (with pre-consecrated Hosts but no priest) for CCD teachers were especially disturbing. A polyester globe (the "Hugg-A-Planet" pillow) replaced the crucifix. There were prayers to "Our Mother" and prayer intentions for "men and boys deluded by false notions of manhood." It was only a matter of time before parishioners were fed up and took the matter to the bishop.

The bishop's response was decisive: Nearly all the parishioners must either submit to a year of group psychotherapy (at their own expense) or the parish would be virtually shut down. Since too few church members were willing to turn themselves over to the straighteners, all Masses, the Sacraments and other organized church functions were forbidden. The bishop's only criticism of the New Age nun was that she went "too fast."[7] No, it was the orthodox members of St. Boniface Catholic Church that needed help. One might ask whether the faithful should have acquiesced in the pagan activities of their sister rather than lose the Church in their community. But we must remember why we come to the Church. We come for spiritual reasons and have very little to lose once the Church has failed in its spiritual purpose.

The struggle is difficult. It is more likely than not that your pastor is open to New Age ideas. Matthew Fox is quoted from the pulpit. Too many bishops are more worried over feminist concerns than they are about the loss of the Faith. Even Catholics with no interest in New Age practices are becoming accustomed to its concepts; they should be well primed if Creation-Centered Spirituality becomes the norm in our churches. But our resistance is neither hopeless nor futile.

We can let others know where we stand. Realistically, it is your brother in the next pew who is most apt to be open to reason. Not having had the benefit of a modernist seminary education, he can rely more on common sense and his or her Catholic upbringing. That is the strongest card to play. Nobody remembers God the Mother from grade school. Nobody used to be taught to visualize demons masquerading as Jesus. Nobody used to minimize Original Sin so as better

---

7. Donna Steichen, "St. Boniface on the Couch: Psychology as Religion, Minnesota-Style," *Fidelity*, September 1989, p. 28.

to celebrate our "Original Blessing."

We must have thicker skins. We must stand, even as others fall around us. If the latest ideas reek of pantheism, the problem is not with our noses. There is nothing wrong with the Gospel that we first learned. Yes, we are often sinful. And unjust. And unkind. But let us not be driven into the inhuman arms of the New Age by the seeming hopelessness of this age. Salvation lies not in the New Age, but where it always has and always will endure: In the merits of Jesus Christ our Lord.

Appendix.

New Age Politics, Economics and Social Change

A Partial Agenda

A weakening of the national government by two means:
- Political decentralization, with power held by regional and local governments.
- Transfer of sovereign national power to a global authority. Many plans for this exist. One is the Constitution for the Federation of the Earth. It provides for a tri-lateral parliament made up of an elected or appointed House of Nations, an elected House of Peoples and a nominated House of Counselors from the world's universities. Also, there would be a world judiciary, a world executive, and of course, a world police force.

Regular transfer payments from industrial to developing countries:
- Third World debt would be converted to outright grants. Aid would be withheld from countries resisting New Age reform.

Sustainable economics:
- Only renewable resources would be developed.

Nations and/or Corporations which use non-renewable resources would pay a severance royalty to compensate for their irresponsibility.

- The automobile would become uncommon. People would move to smaller communities. Twenty percent of us would return to the farm. Mass transit would serve those who remained in the cities.

Appropriate Technology (A.T.), also known as human scale, intermediate or alternate technology:

- A.T. is small, cheap, simple, ecologically benign and sensitive to natural harmonies. It shows a preference for decentralization and nonmaterial values. It is spiritual. Windmills are A.T. Bulldozers are not.

Minimum/Maximum Incomes:

- Everyone would be guaranteed a minimum income. This would free up people who want to develop themselves outside traditional jobs. The income tax would provide for total confiscation of earnings above a certain level. Money should not be a problem because everyone would live under "voluntary simplicity."

Population control:

- It would be necessary to reduce the present world—and U.S.—population by 30% or more. Abortion would remain freely available and tax laws would penalize families with more than their share of children.

Repeal of all compulsory education laws:

- Values education would take priority over basic literacy and math.

Extension of rights to children:
- The rights, duties, and responsibilities of adults would be given to children at much earlier age levels. They would choose to live where and how they wished; whether to be educated or not; to make contracts, collect welfare and engage in sex acts with any partner(s) of their choosing.

Elimination of Crime:
- Crime would immediately be cut in half by repealing half of the criminal laws. All drugs, gambling, prostitution and sexual perversions would be legal.
- Nearly all prisons would be closed, in favor of rehabilitation hostels.

Proper Use of the Media:
- The "fairness doctrine" would be enforced. Authorities would oversee the press to insure against one-sided reporting.
- Advertising of food not deemed healthful would not be permitted.

Abolition of any licensing of health practitioners:
- M.D.'s would be no more legitimate than psychic healers, witch doctors, hypnotists, Indian medicine men, vitamin peddlers and acupuncturists.

Suggested Reading

Note: Some of the authors listed below are Protestant writers. They are offered not for agreement with Catholic teaching, but for their helpfulness in illuminating the New Age Movement.

A Catechism of Modernism, by Rev. J. B. Lemius, O.M.I.
Hidden Dangers of the Rainbow, by Constance Cumbey
A Planned Deception, by Constance Cumbey
A Crisis of Truth, by Ralph Martin
The Seduction of Christianity, by Dave Hunt
Beyond Seduction, by Dave Hunt
Teilhardism and the New Religion, by Wolfgang Smith
The AntiChrist, by Vincent Miceli
The Twisted Cross, by Joseph Carr
Gods of the New Age, by Caryl Matrisciana
Rest from the Quest, by Ellisa Lindsey McClain
The Beautiful Side of Evil, by Johanna Michaelsen
Pascendi Dominic Gregis, by Pope St. Pius X.
Partisans of Error, by Michael Davies
Globalism: America's Demise, by William M. Bowen, Jr.
Original Sin in the Light of Modern Science, by Rev. Patrick O'Connell

If you have enjoyed this book, consider making your next selection from among the following . . .

Prices guaranteed through December 31, 1992.

At your bookdealer or direct from the publisher.

Prices guaranteed through December 31, 1992.